PASSAGE

by

Belva Ann Prycel

Goose River Press
Waldoboro, Maine

Copyright © 2013 Belva Ann Prycel.

All rights reserved. No part of this book may be reproduced in any form without written permission from the publisher, except by a reviewer who may quote brief passages in a review to be printed in a newspaper or magazine.

Library of Congress Card Number: 2013908027

ISBN: 978-1-59713-144-5

First Printing, 2013

Cover painting, "Atlantic Sunrise, Series 2," by Belva Ann Prycel.

Published by
Goose River Press
3400 Friendship Road
Waldoboro ME 04572
e-mail: gooseriverpress@roadrunner.com
www.gooseriverpress.com

Acknowledgements…..

With deep gratitude to Robin and Tom Schmidt,
Kelly Patton Brook, David A. Berry, and Tania Deary,
all who responded deeply to the work with their spirits
and their tears, and to my husband, Lewis,
who was a sympathetic and patient presence
throughout all of the writing and all of the years.

Foreword

The following is the story of a woman's journey, my own, through a time of deep crisis and disillusionment. It is also the story of my family—its courage, foibles, flaws, and moments of grace. In it, I believe, is the story of everyone who has encountered the immense and humbling struggles of life.

When I began to write about this difficult period I intended only to set it down as a personal way of making peace with it, of understanding in order to fully accept what had occurred. Later, I realized that the process became much more than that, and a host of memories and nearly forgotten moments returned to me, spoke to me anew, and found a life on these pages.

The world is rarely what we think it is; it is a malleable entity that alters with our experiences and perceptions, our beliefs and deepest fears. So it was with me. But I have learned that the moments of grace are always with us, always there to lead us back again into the light. For those who have known times of darkness and despair, I offer my story and that of my family as a message of hope.

—Belva Ann Prycel
Sheepscot Village, Maine

Chapter One

I suppose it all began with the phone call. It started there, although it was, in itself, a simple act, and I answered the ringing with no expectations. The Universe was a beneficent place then; it had always been so for me. The immense and deadly stirrings of the world did not veer too dangerously in my direction. I was blessed, and felt I had always been so.

I was an only child, 38, married, and I guess if my life was not ecstatic it was at least predictable. I lived on a lake then, painted landscapes, gardened, and taught art classes in a converted barn on the property. I was also childless, wholly by choice. And you could say that if I was not completely happy, I was at least not unhappy for I lived in the gray area where one defines satisfaction as that state of equilibrium somewhere between sporadic anointings of pleasure and pain. I was content.

I was also deeply loved, a valuable certitude carried in me from childhood. My parents, and my husband, completed a kind of circle of affection in my life. So I was, perhaps, unprepared for the call.

"Yes?" I answer. I am standing at the kitchen window, watching the newly blossomed iris heads topping a brick walk I built the year before, the one which surrounds my perennial bed in front of the lake house. The extravagant purple coifs nod slightly in a little passing breeze.

"Hello. Is this Belva Ann?" a man queries.

"Yes," I reply, recognizing the voice immediately....and

something else, like a deep barely audible undertone, a silence before words, something I couldn't quite wrap my awareness around.

"Yes...?"

"I hope I'm doing the right thing in calling you. I thought that your mother might live alone?"

"No, she lives with my father," I corrected. I think the doctor might have this impression because I was the one who accompanied my mother to his office two weeks before. Mother said she was tired, and she had lost some weight—much more than I realized. When I saw her in the examining room, her legs and arms seemed to have shrunk, yet her eyes in their sockets looked larger. Maybe she was just rundown; after all, she was 74...

"The tests show a mass on the colon, and some shadowy areas on the liver..." Dr. Reiser's voice came across a deep uncertain void.

"What? What do you mean by a mass? You don't think...is it cancer?"

"Yes, I think so. I could even feel something when I was examining her. It appears to be a large tumor...I'm sorry."

"How large? What do you mean? What can we do?" The questions come pouring out of me, a racing torrent of words suddenly making it difficult to get enough air to speak, to breathe.

"I really don't know. We don't know much right now."

"Well, what would you recommend?" I hear my voice quaking.

"I think your mother should see a surgeon as soon as possible. Do you want me to call and tell her?"

"No. No. That's okay. I'll talk to her. I'll tell her."

"I'm so sorry to be giving you this news," he says again.

"I understand. Thank you, Doctor."

I hang up, watching my hand place the phone on its wall receiver, seeing my arm as a detached part of me that operates with a will of its own. Somewhere in the back of my mind a voice, a witness, is noting the hand, feeling the moment, looking at the hand again, knowing this is the moment I will remember in a life, the instant when everything shifted, fell apart, changed. My stomach forms into a knot of pain, one that emanates into my chest, my center. "The heart is the organ of pain." The words come to me, from where I do not remember. The constriction moves up into my throat. I notice my hand still holds the phone, as if I could freeze time, as if I could go back to 3 minutes ago when I first heard it ring, picked it up, and was part of something that doesn't exist anymore. I have slipped into a void. The world shatters. I fall down onto the little wooden bench in the kitchen, the one my husband made, and I wail, "My mother, my mother...Oh God please no, not my mother."

A part of me says this cannot be, cannot happen—not cancer, not again. Not this way. Not after she fought so hard to live. She had beaten it when she was 41, when I was 6 years old. I remember she had been so sick, so deathly ill for such a long time. There were the months of something called radiation. How sick it made her, how weak! I could see her throwing up into a pan on the side of the bed, or laying for days with what she called her "sick headaches." Then she was in a Philadelphia hospital for a month after her surgery. Cousin Aida came to live with my father and me then, in my mother's house, to take her place, to care for me and my father. I hated her, despised her because she wasn't my mother. I was defiant. I was abandoned.

My father had a service station next door but I never saw him until a few minutes before I went to bed. Aida would give him a report on my misbehavior, and he would sternly correct me. It seemed he was close by, but he wasn't really there. He worked all the time then, maybe to avoid talking to Aida, maybe to avoid dealing with me.

I saw my mother only once during that time she was in the hospital. Children were not allowed visitation privileges then, but my father and my mother's cousin Mina snuck me up to her floor on a service elevator. I remember seeing her at the end of a long hall in a wheelchair, seemingly waiting for us. I ran to her down the shiny tiled gray floor. We were both crying, but she was alive. She was going to be okay.

The doctors said she was a miracle. No one had ever survived a cancer so advanced. She said it was because she *had* to live: she had a little girl to raise. And this she did, and 33 years had passed.

I wipe my eyes and look at the irises that had wavered in the wind so gracefully just moments before. Why did they look so different, so insignificant now? The garden itself was a diminishment, an artifice of superficiality, color and form that meant nothing. It no longer pleases me to look at it.

I stare back at the phone. I cannot call Lew, my husband. He is at work, probably in a class now. I don't want to tell Mother anything. Not yet. I want to talk to her in a way that doesn't frighten her as it has me. She will need surgery, probably. And some kind of treatment. Chemotherapy? Even the word makes me feel sick. Can she handle it? Will she be able to stay strong enough for any treatment? She has already lost a lot of weight. Maybe the doctors won't be able to operate. My mind races ahead, weighing possibilities. "Stop!" says the witness in my head. It is pointless to anticipate. There isn't a firm diagnosis. I don't know enough. Still.....Doctor Rieser's call was so frightening, apologetic, as though the tumor was very large, as though—I cannot go there now. I cannot think.

I reach for the phone to call my father. He needs to know this. We will talk together, then decide how to tell Mother.

I dial the number through a blur of tears, by muscle memory. I am glad when my father answers. I cannot repress sobs as I tell him what I know. I recall that I say we need to talk about this, we need to decide how to tell Mother. I assume she is somewhere nearby because he has no response except, "Okay, okay, honey. I'll be coming up right now." The call is over.

"What did Belva Ann want?" my mother asks.

"The doctor called and says you have cancer. Belva Ann's upset and I have to go." My father turns and leaves.

***

"He said that? How could he do that? How could he say that to you, then just walk away?" I ask. My mother is telling me what happened. She is feeling hopeless, dealing with this alone.

I am incredulous, staggered by the insensitivity of it, of my father. She is lying on the wicker sofa and I hold her. We are both crying. I apologize for my father. I tell her it is not the bleak picture she is seeing. There are treatments, surgeries, medications. This is not the same thing that she faced years ago. More can be done now. We will get through this, together.

"Oh, Belva Ann, I never thought this would happen to me again. I don't know. I just thought I was tired and needed some vitamins," she smiles at her naivete. "That's what I thought the doctor would say." She is rubbing her forehead, fighting back more tears. I see her as so much younger than 74. She is vibrant looking, active, always having friends over for dinner, volunteering at the hospital, baking cookies for the local kids who stop by to say hello to her. She is the neighborhood grandmother to all of them. Her beautiful face is surrounded by a crown of brown wavy hair. There is almost no gray in it. She looks too young to be sick.

"Look, Mommy. Daddy had no right to tell you that way. I don't know what he was thinking. That is *not* what the doctor said. He said you have a tumor. It needs to be removed. They don't even know for sure if it's cancer, but if it is, cancer can be treated. Lots of people live years with cancer. We just don't know exactly what we're dealing with yet." I was trying to string words together in a way that left some openings for hope. And why not? None of us knew anything for sure.

"I don't know" she wondered. "I should have known something was wrong. I didn't like the barium enema. I told the doctor in the hospital I would never have that again. Your father didn't want to wait around the hospital so I drove myself."

I shook my head in more disbelief. "Mother....you should have called me. I would have taken you."

"I didn't want to bother you. You have your classes and I thought I would be all right. But they puff you up with all this chalky liquid, and then they keep telling you, "Drink, drink more." They put more chalk, or barium, in you and they puff you up with gas. I told them they had to stop. I was miserable. I had had enough."

"What happened then?" I asked.

She sighed. "They finally finished and said they had enough pictures, and I got dressed. It was all I could do to walk to the parking lot. I had all this barium dribbling out onto my shoes. I didn't think I could make it home. I just kept passing it for a long time. I was so exhausted."

I felt, again, angry at my father for letting her go through this alone, but I held my tongue. "Well, I'm glad that's over now, but I'm so sorry that I wasn't there to help you. I can tell you you'll never get rid of me again. And it is going to be okay. We are all going to get through this." I say the same phrases over and over, as if by repetition I can make them reality. I am worried, but I'm not about to let her lose all hope.

She is rising off the couch and changing the subject. "Come on. I've made some good soup. You always liked vegetable soup."

***

Back at the lake I am treading water, paddling just beyond our dock, the old pier under an overhanging maple tree. The lake is stained with cedar tannins, golden brown, like weak tea. I drop below the surface and hang suspended, floating on half a lungful of air, ejecting tiny bubbles which rise through the water like pearls. I think of nothing. Out here I am fish, unattached to the land. The water ensorcells me, supports me.

The last few weeks have torn me emotionally. I have been sick with worry about Mother. The pain in my chest and stomach will not leave. I am glad my classes are over, that it is summer, that I can concentrate on helping her.

We have an appointment with the surgeon in the afternoon and I meet my parents at their house. My father insists on driving. It takes awhile to find a parking space, then longer sitting in the waiting room. After Mother goes in to the examining room, I wait with my father in another inner office, feeling the sterility of the white walls, the colorless row of diplomas, the hardness of the ceramic floor, the straight-backed wooden chairs. The doctor comes out and talks to us as Mother gets dressed. He is thin, in his late sixties, sandy-haired and pale, also humorless and awkwardly direct.

"I'm afraid she's very sick," he says, looking at my father, then at me. "She has a very large tumor in the colon, and maybe some secondary tumors on the liver. It is not good."

My father looks uncomprehending, almost childlike.

"I can operate on the colon. I think we should do that. Otherwise her bowel could become obstructed....then we'll see...maybe chemotherapy."

My father says nothing. He seems numbed. The whole thing is too much for him to take in.

Mother joins us then and the doctor repeats some of what he has said to us, leaving out the size of the tumor or the possible involvement of the liver. He says he'll be able to give a better prognosis after he has seen exactly what is going on "inside."

Mother shakes her shoulders and tells him she has had cancer once before. She asks if he knows Dr. McFaden, her surgeon at Hahnemann Hospital. "But of course," she says, "that was many years ago. He's probably not even practicing now." She looks away, wistful. "I will have to think about the surgery awhile," she says.

"Yes, you should think it over," the doctor replies. "Just call the office when you're ready and I'll set it up." He pauses and taps a pen on the desk, "But I do advise you not to wait too long."

"I understand," Mother replies, looking at her hands.

We leave the office, down a wheelchair exit ramp and onto the sidewalk. No one says anything. I have Mother's arm. We cross the street and get into the car. My father fidgets with the keys and talks about the trouble he had finding a parking place here. It is a suburb of one-way streets, and he made 3 or 4 circuits of the block till a space opened up. Now he must head about again in the opposite direction to get home.

"There was nothing anywhere in this place. I had to go around and around. You'd think they'd make some parking places somewhere. They've got the streets all bollixed up..."

Dear God, I think, my mother has just been told that she has cancer, and my father can speak of nothing but parking difficulties?

"John, I think we have some bigger things to deal with now," my mother says, near tears.

I am in the back seat, feeling as I did at 6 or 7, rubbing both of them on the shoulders, trying to make it somehow okay. "We'll get through this," I keep repeating, not knowing how to be, not having any better words to offer. We are each in our separate thoughts as we drive home, but I keep my hand on my mother's shoulder. I don't want to let go.

***

It is Memorial Weekend. Why does everything happen on Memorial Weekend? Two summers before I had a hysterectomy on this date; before that, an Emergency Room visit in terrible pain from a rampant infection. Now mother's surgery is scheduled for a few days before the holiday. The weather has been intolerably hot. It is the start of summer and I wonder what lies ahead.

I have drawings in the studio and I work on them less now as art, than as a form of therapy. Occasionally I become so engrossed that I forget the surrounding anxiety for a time. I turn to renderings, detailed studies of shells, plants, common objects, and they help to focus my attention on the reality of the moment, the intricacies of the observer and the observed. If I were of Eastern persuasion, perhaps I could meditate; if an athlete, I would run. As it is, my fingers, my eyes, make the extensions for me. This is the only comfort I find now, the only time the knot in my stomach eases.

The textured illustration board slides under the edge of the pencil catching the shading, the form, the patterns of the weave. I work on the drawing from the lightest tone, to the dark. Will the months ahead be like this, I wonder, with indistinct gray areas, indeterminate patterns slipping gradually into black? I put down the pencil and cannot finish now.

She had her surgery two days ago. I sat with my father for three hours in a roomful of anxious people, all waiting for news of a loved one sequestered in a surgery somewhere beyond those soundless walls. The doctors always came out and spoke to the families afterwards. I tried to hear what they were saying, feeling a kinship with all of them, and an isolation at the same time. A deep mystical part of me wanted the news to be good, believed it would be, held it as a prayer, a hope.

Perhaps they could remove the disease. Mother wanted it gone, wanted the tumor out of her body. It was an invader, vile, and I saw it being taken out and discarded in some ugly hospital bag. Cast out. She would feel better then. She could be treated, helped.

I had been there since early morning at first light. I had

sat in the room as the nurses prepped her. She said she was not afraid, that whatever happened, she was at peace. She just hoped they "could get it all." I told her it was good that she was having the surgery. I believed she would feel better after she got through this. I tried to put some visions of pleasant things ahead. I told her she would have the summer to recover, and we could sit on the dock she loved at the lake and watch the sunsets and swim and talk. I gave her a card with a picture of the dock and our poodle Enjoué, Mother's pal and swimming companion. It said "Your Dock and Mascot Await." It was something to hold, I hoped, to look forward to.

The orderlies came and took her as I held her hand. We went down the elevator and paused a moment outside the operating room. As they took her away, we kissed goodbye and both smiled. She was groggy then and lifted her hand weakly in a wave. I turned to the waiting area, and the tears came then, a monsoon, from the eyes, nose, mouth. I felt the wetness fall on my sandaled feet. No...I could not do this.

I snuffed and blew my nose and went to get a cup of coffee in the cafeteria, wishing for the first time in a long time that I had a cigarette. I had given them up the year before. But this day, I wanted one desperately. No, the coffee would have to do.

Near noontime Father appeared. He looked haggard and had not eaten anything, and we sat together and said little. Our eyes were fixed on the wall clock, and on each subtle movement of the door, the rattle of a passing gurney, or a sound of footsteps in the hall.

In mid-afternoon when Dr. Davitz finally appeared he seemed reluctant to see us. He stood five feet away, performing what seemed an unpleasant requirement of his duties. I tried to meet his eyes but he looked instead at some distant point in the room. "She came through it about as well as could be expected," he said. "I did as much as I could, but as I thought, the tumor was quite large and I removed a section of the colon. I could see some tumors on the liver but we can't remove those."

"You mean it's metastasized?" I asked.

"Yes. And I could see small cancers in the peritoneal area. It looked like someone had thrown a handful of rice in there."

"This sounds pretty bad," said my father.

"I'm sorry, yes."

"How long could she have?" I asked then.

"I don't know. We can't know these things for sure."

There was a long pause. Finally I said, "Doctor Davitz, I understand you're not a prophet, but you're a doctor and must have some idea. We need to know so we can plan what to do. Surely you have a sense of it."

He looked disgusted, miffed rather than dismayed—or devastated as we were.

"Okay," he sighed. It could possibly be as long as six months, could be only two months. No, I doubt it would be six months, although I really can't say for sure. Everyone's different."

There was no emotion, no compassion expressed. And I could see he hated being cornered with these questions, hated being unable to just leave the room having performed his basic task. Then turning to me, irritated, he leveled a final shot. "Look, if you'd brought Mother to me sooner, I could have done something."

My head reeled: *If I'd brought Mother...not "my mother," not "your mother," but some non-specific, simply generic mother...then he could have helped her? Or if "I" had brought Mother, rather than herself, or my father bringing her...then she could have been saved?*

Thus stated I had failed her. The responsibility was mine.

***

My father and I left the hospital wordlessly that day, each

in our own grief and shock. Mother would be sedated for the rest of the day, so there was no need to remain. I spoke to Social Services and hired a private duty nurse to be in her room for the first two nights. Knowing how little attention one receives in an overburdened hospital, I thought the presence of a qualified professional nurse would be comforting. Also having my own great fear and intolerance to pain, I needed to be assured that Mother would be kept comfortable.

The next afternoon when I returned, I was surprised to find her sitting up, alert. She wanted to see the doctor, to know what he found. An orderly came by and brought some ginger ale and a snack of carrots and celery. It seemed an odd dietary choice to me, inappropriate for someone who had just undergone a bowel resection. I went out to the nurse's station.

"My mother...the patient down the hall...she's just had intestinal surgery, and she's down there eating celery. Does that seem right to you?" I asked.

"Oh no, it doesn't," said the nurse, pulling her chart. "She should only have clear liquids."

"Good God, then you'd better get down there," I screamed.

We both ran back to the room, grabbing the half-eaten celery from my mother's hand.

"These go to the patient next door, "the nurse panted. "You can keep the soda though. Sorry about the mistake."

I was stunned and about to issue forth on the ineptitude of the hospital when Dr. Rieser suddenly appeared in the doorway. "Everything okay? How are you doing Mrs. Penn?" He was coming around the bed and took her hand in his quiet, gentle way.

"Is there anything you need?" he asked.

"Well, she doesn't need celery and carrots," I said abysmally shaken about the lack of vigilance on the part of the hospital...but Mother had other issues on her mind.

"No, I'm doing all right, Doctor. I'm just waiting to see Dr.

Davitz. I hope he was able to get it all." Her voice was soft and hoarse.

"Yes," he said. "That would be good. And if you keep doing this well, you may be able to go home in a few more days."

"I would like that. I guess none of us like a hospital, do we?"

He smiled and said he'd be checking in on her when he made his rounds, and we walked out into the hallway and down to the sitting room at the end of the corridor. I had no control over my emotions and began to cry again. It seemed to be all I was doing of late, but he had been my doctor for so long and I felt I almost knew him as a friend.

"The surgeon said it's very bad. He said if he'd seen Mother sooner, he could have helped her. I feel I've let her down...and now..." I began to sob.

He put his hand on my arm and shook me lightly. "No, don't think that. You can't always know what's happening. Sometimes, when you see someone everyday, the changes are so small that you don't notice. I can see someone who's cancer free one week, and the next week they have cancer. Some diseases don't present with symptoms until they're very far advanced. No one, not even doctors, can be God."

I looked at his calm brown eyes, humility and concern emanating from their depths. He was a physician who treated the spirit as well as the body, who had no lofty illusions of his powers but who cared deeply for his patients and their families. Mother hadn't even been his patient till I brought her to see him a few weeks ago. Her own doctor, I felt, had been dismissive of her for years. As I talked to Doctor Rieser, the burden of guilt I'd accepted for the last day lifted off me.

"Let me see if I can talk to Dr. Davitz, find out exactly what he saw. I'll get back to you, I promise."

I knew he would, knew if there were any remnants of information that might help us Dr. Rieser would seek them out. He had already helped me more than he could know. I hugged him then and returned to Mother's room where I found her sleeping, the half-empty soda glass next to her bed. She looked very small and fragile, a brown sparrow connected to a nest of tubes and lines. I kissed her cheek and tiptoed out.

***

The house was dark, quiet, but I was awake, listening. Beside me Lew softly snored as I rose from the bed, trying not to disturb him. I needed something to help me sleep and my head ached. I went down the stairs for a glass of milk. Outside, through the double windows in the dining room I could see the silhouette of the iron fountain with the ibis atop it, and over that, the faint glimmer of a path made by the moon on the lake. I opened the door and followed it across the darkened yard, out onto the dock. Two old wooden folding chairs faced the water, the ones that Mother and I had sat in just days before.

"You turn around," she said, "and your children are gone. You turn around again, and you're 70 and your life is gone...and you wonder...where did it go?"

The lake, the shushing shore, the moon, compound the silence. Somewhere from the direction of Richman's barn an owl calls, "Who? Who?"

Who? I thought. All of us. As transient as last year's maple leaves crusting the bottom of the lake, as indefinable as water vapor shifting to clouds, falling in ribbons of rain that fed the somnolent cedar stream. It was all so fleeting, so indefinable.

***

A week had gone by and still the surgeon did not stop to see her, a week of avoidance and awkward pauses. We were all forced to be co-conspirators, lying by feigning ignorance, forced into complicity because we didn't want to jeopardize her frail recovery. It was, in some way irresponsible, this lack of communication, of pretending to be cheerful, of self-monitoring every intonation, every facial expression, but I knew if the surgeon didn't tell her, we would have to do it soon.

As it happened, the day of her release, Dr. Davitz stopped by the room. He told her, probably in the most oblique way, he "hadn't been able to get everything." He was recommending chemotherapy, but she should wait a few weeks, until she was stronger. I don't know what else he said, if anything, but Mother felt he had been wrong to keep this from her. Perhaps we were all wrong, although I was only able to feel glad that she was coming home, that she had survived surgery, that we still had some time together..

My father vacuumed the house on the day of her release and I prepared a simple supper of chicken and vegetables. The neighbors came with a pan of lasagna. Uncle Bob and Aunt Mary Emma, mother's cousin and his wife who lived just one block away, stopped by with a cake and a bouquet of summer flowers. Cards filled the house from friends and neighbors, some who stopped to welcome her home, to inquire as to how she was feeling. She put up a good face, but I could see it was exhausting her and I tried to ease them out, saying she needed to rest. It was my father however who seemed to need the attention more.

"I'm not well either" he blurted as some neighbors were leaving. "You know, me legs hurt, and me back, and I can't get me breath sometimes." He rubbed his chest and grimaced as if to emphasize the point. "So Belva's not the only one's got problems."

"Daddy, I didn't know you were feeling that bad," I said, concerned.

"Well, I've got these knots here," he said, pulling up his pant leg for the assembled well-wishers, exposing some thick purple varicose veins. "And I've lost weight too. Look at me belt"...he stood up and pushed his thumb between the pants and belt buckle stretched to a gap of three or four inches, then made a show of hitching in the excess fabric using the last hole in the loop.

Then looking at me pointedly, "Your mother's not well, but I don't feel so good either." He shook his shoulders.

I felt embarrassed, as I so often had as a kid, as a young woman, a sensation that came back to me from some nearly forgotten territory of the past. I got up to heat the dinner, leaving him to carry on his complaints to others.

"Geez," Lew said, following me into the kitchen. "He acts like he's jealous because your mother's getting all the attention."

"I know," I replied, "what a way to get attention, by getting cancer."

Chapter Two

Summer was marked by heat, daily trips to see Mother and Father, the lake, doctors, and a visit from my mother's cousin Mina. From childhood I remembered her as a loving, intelligent, and compulsive woman who after a brief unhappy marriage, spent the remainder of her life alone. An elementary school teacher, Mina had been morbidly obese in her youth, but by sheer will and relentless self-denial had withered herself down to a manageable, if not petite, 150 pounds. This she had accomplished by vigilance, manipulation, and thoroughly neurotic fixation. She cooked with an absence of oil, fat, or butter and used a sweetener called saccharin, something that found its way into every food and which left an acrid, bitter, metallic aftertaste. The meals for the guests she occasionally entertained were portion-controlled by being served in left-over plastic TV dinner trays. Likewise holiday meals were prepared ahead, frozen, and dispensed in the same manner.

As if control of food wasn't compulsive enough, she was equally fixated on cleanliness. No dust ball, pet hair, or other unclean object ever survived in Mina's apartment. My mother, a fastidious housekeeper, was no match for Mina, and I suppose this is why she found it difficult to have her as a houseguest. So when Mina, deeply distressed by Mother's illness, announced she was coming for a visit in July, I immediately offered to have her stay with us.

My dog Enjoué boisterously greeted Cousin Mina as she arrived from the airport with two huge bags the size of sofa cushions, each weighing over 50 pounds. My husband had one in each hand and his arms appeared to have gained a few inches in length and sweat stood on his brow.

"I've probably brought more clothes than I need," she said apologizing, "but you never know what the weather's going to be like up here. Last year I froze. But I guess I've gotten used to Florida weather and can't take the North."

She had gotten smaller since I last saw her, an aspect of the constant dieting no doubt, combined with the natural shrinkage of skin with age, like clothes that have been left in the dryer too long. She was dressed immaculately for the visit, with a neat little matching violet jacket and skirt, bright scarf, earrings, a flashy rhinestone pin, and coordinated shoes with a tiny purple leather strap that perfectly matched the suit.

As I looked at her I remembered coming upon Mina's shoe closet years ago and being stunned by over fifty pairs of shoes all lined up like soldiers in upright metal stands.

"I like this pair," she had said, holding up some pretty pumps with open toes. They looked small to me however, and I knew Mina wore a size 10.

"Oh, I know they're a size 7," she remarked casually, intuiting the unspoken question in my mind, "But they were on sale and such a good buy that I couldn't pass them up."

"Oh," I nodded, as if this somehow explained it.

Now I saw her, dressed for her visit with fastidious exactitude, but with a face full of worry and concern. She loved my mother greatly, and me, and I grabbed her and kissed a rouged cheek and told her how happy I was to see her. I meant it with all my heart.

"I want to know about your mother," she said as soon as she unpacked her vast wardrobe and got settled in. I told her the basics of what I knew and assured her that Mother was doing okay for now, that she and Father would be coming up to the lake tomorrow. She could spend some time with Mother on the dock while I took Daddy to see a cardiologist in nearby Elmer.

"What? Your father's having heart problems?" she asked, surprised.

"I don't know, Mina. I just know that he's complaining of chest pains and is not getting any real medical help from his GP, the same doctor he and Mother have had for years who has done nothing. So I decided to make an appointment for him to see a specialist.

Look, do you believe this?" I said, reaching for a paper on the counter. "This is the entire medical record for my father from a doctor he has had for 40 years." I held up a single page with two sentences which listed his current medications— there was no medical history, no information on surgeries, no past or recent test results, nothing.

"This is a sham" I said, throwing the page on the kitchen table. I had seen enough of the medical profession by then to develop a skepticism and general disdain for doctors.

"Harry Day," said Mina. That was the closest she ever came to swearing, but she was as incredulous as I was. "Well, it's good you'll be taking him to see someone tomorrow."

"I have to, Mina. He can't fall apart now, not when Mother is needing him so much."

***

The next day I am sitting with my father in the office of Doctor Silva. He is a middle-aged, handsomely attired man with an ease and an elegance in his demeanor. He studies my father's tests...

"Well, Mr. Penn. You have some angina, as you know, and I can give you some nitro tablets to help with that, but I don't see anything in your EKG or stress test that raises any major concern. There's an occasional irregular heart beat, but it's what we consider benign and nothing to worry about."

The doctor is talking to my father who sits half naked on the examining table, passive as a frightened child, amazingly vulnerable and unquestioning.

"You mean my ticker's okay, Doctor?" my father asks, disbelieving.

"I would say so, yes...now, you could stand to lose a little weight, but you're doing well for, let's see...seventy-seven? Yes?" My father nods. "And we have some newer medications that can help with the symptoms you're having. Also I'll write you a prescription for a mild anti-anxiety medication. I'd like to see you in two weeks to see how you're doing."

"Thank you, Doctor," my father says, smiling broadly then shaking Dr. Silva's hand. He is relieved. For years he has been convinced he has something terrible and would see no doctor other than his incompetent and aged GP. Now he has amazingly good news, and as we drive back to the lake he talks about how wonderful Dr. Silva is, how thorough, how he "seems to know his stuff." Then, after the glowing monologue, the conversation abruptly changes to Mother.

"You know, I can't seem to do a thing that pleases her. It's always 'get this John,' 'do that John,' and you know, I tell her 'Belva, I've only got two arms and two legs. I can't do everything at once.' "

"That must be hard. Would you like to have a home health aide, maybe someone to do some errands, help around the house some? I could check into that for you."

"Naaaw...your mother wouldn't want anyone in her house. She wants to do everything herself, or have me do it."

"Well, Daddy, she's still cooking and shopping, isn't she? Doing most of the things she did before the surgery? Maybe I can help. I could stop down more so you could get out and do a few things. Or Lew could help."

"Naaaw," again, "we're okay," and I sensed he really didn't want the help yet. "It's just that nothin' I do ever suits her. You know how she is."

He looked at me for confirmation, but I said nothing, just

kept driving, thinking how familiar it all seemed, even in the midst of crisis and tragedy—the bickering, the complaints, the patterns of a lifetime which persisted. I stupidly thought there'd be some sort of transformation, a rising to the occasion, that the old battles for control would pale in the reality of the situation we faced. I am barely internalizing that this is not the case. I don't know why I am surprised, but I am.

My parents' marriage was always turbulent, full of loud argument and disagreement, of conflicts that were never directly resolved. Yet I knew that neither of them had ever been unfaithful or considered leaving the marriage. Emotionally they were as distant, I guessed, as a man and a woman could be, yet they were committed to remaining together. Maybe it had to do with diminishing expectations; maybe it was the structure of the social culture in which they had been raised. I didn't know, hadn't considered it much until now when as an adult I could see them as individuals and not just as my parents.

I couldn't ruminate on this for too long for we were crossing the lake and I could see Mother and Mina seated on the two chairs, facing west, probably seeing the car as we approached. They would be anxious to know what Dr. Silva said.

It was a cool July afternoon as we came down the green lawn to the little dock. Mother turned, "Well, how did it go?" she asked.

Father bubbled with his good news, his mood entirely altered, now ebullient as he described all the impressive qualities of Dr. Silva and announced his improved bill of health. I watched, again, with a sense of disbelief bordering on reproach. Couldn't he at least low key the news, refrain from such complete elation? Couldn't he consider how this must feel to my mother whose own prognosis had been so terrible? I watched it all, reacting silently, feeling that all the emotional self-absorptions of the past were nothing compared to this. When he was done, Mina said, "That's really wonderful, John."

My mother looked across the lake, eyes full in the afternoon sun, "Yes, such good news," she said, then a pause..."I only wish that mine had been as good."

At that moment my heart broke, and I felt my perception subtly shift. I felt angry, very angry at my father.

***

"Harry Day! There's a big bug on the stairs!"

It was Mina, and she was already becoming acquainted with the insect life of the North. "And this morning I had a horsefly buzzing in my bedroom!"

"Yes?" I said, making tea, surreptitiously removing one of Enjoué's dog hairs from the rim of the cup. "Well, we live on a lake and I guess we have some insects here you know." Mother would have been dismayed but I simply found Mina's fixations amusing.

She stood in the doorway, dressed as though she were going to a ball, pink silk blouse and pink polyester pants and pink glass beaded necklace and pink high-heeled sandals, size ten.

"Well, don't you look nice," I said, changing the subject and admiring her cool pressed pinkness. She always made me smile.

"I wanted to look good for lunch," she said, twisting the beads coquettishly in her pale hands. "I want to take you all somewhere nice."

We were heading for the shore, to Sea Isle, the town of my parents' old summer house, one that I loved as a kid. I wanted to show them the apartment that Lew and I had rented there for a week in early August, for my parents and ourselves. It was situated right on the beach, with a gorgeous deck and view of the ocean, and it had cost us a great deal, but Lew and I wanted to give them both something special to look forward to. After showing them the rental we were going to a well known restaurant for a seafood lunch.

We had an old Volkswagon van which served me well as an art vehicle. Lew had removed the two back rows of seats and today we put some folding aluminum chairs in the back for everyone. It was something like a beach party back there. My father, a wonderful tenor from his barbershop quartet days, began to sing, "Let Me Call You Sweetheart," to which I joined in "I'm in love with you...," and together we finished the song, ending in a dramatic flourish of harmony. From there, the songfest just continued, most of it the old songs from the thirties and forties, ones which he and I knew so well. I had heard them on every vacation and car trip ever taken when my father broke into song. The words were indelibly imprinted in all their lyrical variations upon my young brain.

Once in awhile, on a familiar round, like "Row Your Boat," Mother and Mina would chime in, not very good singers, but very good appreciators. Lew drove and tapped his hand on the wheel, providing some small background percussion as he was functionally incapable of carrying a tune.

And so we went, talking and singing, with Mother enjoying the little excursion. She had been doing well of late.

Her chemotherapy had started, a mild treatment and something she did once every three weeks. She had not been sick afterwards, but she said she did feel tired for a few days. Otherwise she said she had no discomfort, although she was continuing to lose weight and had become quite thin.

We had a lovely lunch which Mother seemed to be able to enjoy, and on the way home we stopped at a small Methodist church on Route 9. It was one which Mina remembered attending as a young girl when she went to a camp meeting not far from there. The grounds were landscaped in lovely perennials with a pond and bridge and small gazebo next to the water. I watched them walk arm in arm while my father and Lew talked together in the car. Mina and Mother had been friends since girlhood, almost like sisters, and now they looked so old and frail. I walked into the empty church where a piano sat in a corner of the vestibule. I began to play Mina's favorite hymn........"I come to the garden alone, when the dew is still on the roses...." The notes floated out the open doors and over the gentle pond. I wanted to give them this moment together. I heard Mina's soprano voice in my head, singing as she had done so many years ago from the church in Sea Isle. I held the moment in my mind as the two of them sat, sisters still, in the quietude of a fading light.

***

I hated to see Mina go. She had been a good confidante and listener, to me and my parents. Her worry was an aspect of her caring, the equal and opposite dimension of her love. Having her around for the week had somehow lightened my own burden, and I knew she was a comforting presence for Mother and Father. She knew them so well. She had been there when my grandmother, whom I never knew, had been killed in a car crash when Mother was barely 16. They had been standing on the side of the road, talking to friends in a car, when a driver lost control and slammed into them, throwing my mother to the side as her own mother took the full force of the collision, pinned against the other vehicle. She died in less than a day. Mina sat up all night with my mother after this death, holding her in grief. It was a bond they shared in a moment of sorrow, and it lasted for life.

Later, when Mother married, Mina and her husband accompanied the newlyweds on their honeymoon in the White Mountains. I could still see them in old black and white photos, looking young, beautiful, or handsome against the frame of rocky summits and rustic mountain cabins.

I saw Mina now on the concourse of Philadelphia Airport, wearing another perfectly coordinated outfit that appeared from the voluminous depths of her luggage, and waving goodbye sadly as she turned to board the plane. Her hair, once golden brown, was silver and she looked like a pale little white bird hidden under the plumage of over-bright clothing. She was crying and her rouge was running, and I knew that she felt she might not see my mother again. I waved back to her and tried not to cry too. I promised I would call her, every Sunday, to let her know how we were doing.

I stood awhile at the huge windows and watched as her plane taxied out on the runway, then lifted and became airborne. Some part of me wished I were going with her. I was frightened, apprehensive about what might lie ahead. I prayed our week at the coast would go well and I tried to fix my attention on that, dismissing everything else from my mind.

***

The first week in August came upon us quickly. I was glad to be able to do something that didn't involve doctors, medicines, or constant phone calls from my parents' friends. I packed for Lew and myself, got enough food together for the first few days, then stopped at my parents' house to help Mother pack her clothes. As we spread items on the bed my father appeared in the doorway.

"I don't know what I'm going to wear," he said.

I looked at him, frankly wondering what his next difficulty would be, what other service he might require.

"I don't have any shorts," he said, looking helpless.

"Daddy, you *never* wear shorts." I stared back, disgruntled or bemused.

"Just take a couple short-sleeved shirts and your khaki pants," said Mother, sighing, obviously tired.

"Well...I don't know which ones. Nothing fits me anymore," he persisted.

I stared at the checked blue and white shirt in Mother's suitcase, the one she so often wore when she hung laundry, or cleaned house. It was a workshirt, and I found it inexplicably poignant as she had placed it there, this humble and familiar bit of clothing; I wanted to hold it then, to bury my face in it.

"Just pack what you want," she said. "No one dresses up or cares what you wear at the beach."

He slumped away, but when I finished with Mother I went into my father's room and pulled a few items from his closet, laying them on a chair. He opened a drawer and began rummaging around in the underwear.

"Look at me socks," he said.

I hated how he used "me" instead of "my" whenever he wanted sympathy.

"I'm the only man I know who can put his socks on from either end." He stuck his hand through the gap and wriggled his fingers where the toes might go to emphasize the point.

I started to laugh then. "Well, Daddy, we'll have to get you a needle and thread and you can mend them while you're watching the waves break on the coast!"

"Yeh," he said, "or I'll make 'em into some chum bags to attract the sharks."

I smiled and put my hand on his shoulder. "Okay. We'll get you some new socks at the department store in Sea Isle. We're going to have a good week. Don't worry about it."

"I don't know," he said, looking troubled. "Your mother just lays on the sofa all the time, and she's not herself—not herself."

"Look, she's tired," I said. "It's the cancer. That's how it is. They told us she'd be tired. Remember?"

"Yeh—but she's just not herself anymore."

I wondered about that, but didn't allow myself the luxury of reflection. "None of us are, Daddy. It's a hard thing. We need to help her as much as we can, both of us."

He looked at me, and I felt that he was descending into some childlike realm, some place where he could escape all this, and I wondered, had it always been so? Or was I just seeing it more now? Was he really so insensitive, so self-centered? Or was he just terrified, old, and becoming more and more dependent?

I didn't have time to dwell on it however. There was too much to do. Maybe too, I didn't want to see. Maybe I too, wanted to forget.

***

The moon rose full over the ocean, at first a thin rim of light, but one that expanded into a huge orb, casting a smooth sheen of liquid gold on the water. We all stood at the deck railing and watched the moon's ascent, the sounds of the waves rhythmically brushing on the beach below.

My parents loved the coast, and it was for this that I had brought them here.

Mother stood transfixed. "The old moon..." she said, "remember those nights when we used to walk the beach, with the path of the moon following beside us? The old moon path, and no matter where you are, it leads to everyone."

Father began to sing..."By the light, of the silvery moon..." I joined in with him and he immediately took a harmony part as together we finished the little impromptu duet. Mother and Lew allowed us our informal concert on the deck.

"Would you like to follow 'the old moonpath' again?" I asked. "It's a beautiful night."

I was looking at Mother, but the question was directed to all.

"No" she said, a little wistfully. "I'm afraid I might fall. I'm not so steady on my feet in the dark. You and Lew go on. It's nice for your father and me here on the deck."

I turned hand in hand with Lew to stroll the beach, feeling glad that we had such a wonderful spot where they could enjoy the shore, the sunrises and moonrises, the salt breezes in comfort and privacy.

Mother seemed to prefer the early morning for a beach

walk, before the summer bathers appeared, and I would accompany her, gathering shells and polished stones left behind by the tide. For much of the time she sat on a lounge chair on the deck with my father. Often Bob and Mary drove down and joined them, and Lew and I would hear their laughter and conversation wafting down to the beach below.

At these times I was grateful for moments with Lew, or time alone. I struggled to live in the present, treasuring any good moments, but it was as though I was carrying a stone—a boulder—in my chest. It pulled me down from the center of my throat to the space where I presumed a heart should be. It was a weight—there was no other word for it—an anticipatory grieving, a knowing that this was the last summer, the last time on the ocean, the last walks on the beach...the last....

I remembered how, long ago, she would sit with her chair at the edge of the sea, reading as her feet were washed by waves. I saw her there as the child I was, riding my inflatable raft, trying to reach her feet on the remnants of the last wave.

"Oooh, a crab!" she would say as I grabbed her toes.

Soon there would be no wave reaching her, no wave or moonpath, effort or device. She would be as distant as a fallen star, and the pain of this knowledge was almost unbearable to me.

I wondered how it was for her, how it was to know you are losing everything? She spoke of it little, and when she did it was as an eventuality, like rain. She said she worried about me, and especially about my father.

"He's doing an awful lot of surmising," she said one evening as we sat talking, the TV drowning out our voices to Lew and my father in the adjacent kitchen.

"What do you mean?" I asked.

"I mean that, oh, I don't know, he thinks that this person said something, or another is doing something—and he surmises that they think this or that. I told him, 'John, you're doin' a lot of surmising.'"

I didn't know what to make of it, and I still wasn't sure what she meant. "Maybe he needs more to do, something he enjoys. He hasn't gone to the beach once, not even to walk— but then, he never liked it on the beach. He always wanted to be in his boat, or on the bay. Maybe he and Lew could do some clamming. Would he like that?"

"Yes," she brightened, "I think so. Ask him."

My father had always liked to fish as a younger man, and he had owned a series of small powerboats, my favorite being the Lyman lapstrake that he had when I was a teenager. We would leave in the early morning as the first rose-colored light streamed over the crests of the waves, trolling the bay for perch or weakfish, or catching an occasional unwelcome skate or dogshark. I never liked the catching of the fish, but I loved being on the water in the transcendent light, and the companionship with my father. In later years, when he had no boat, he took to clamming, wading and raking in the shallows, dragging a fishnet stretched over an innertube to hold the clams. My father always enjoyed being *around* ocean water; but he was infinitely more at home being *in* the bay.

The next day Lew got the requisite clam rakes and nets together as if by some unknown wizardry. He was able, it seemed, to quietly and almost effortlessly accomplish any requests. I marveled at his steadiness, his reliability, his supportive calm. I was leaning on him more and more emotionally, transitioning to sharing with him the trivial events and intimacies that I had once shared with Mother. In small ways she was detaching.

That night I made clam chowder. Bob and Mary joined us for dinner and my father was exuberant, describing Ludlam's Bay, the feel again of the clam rake on the muddy bottom, the size of some of the bivalves that he and Lew procured. It reminded me of the old days when all of them were at the beach, when Bob and Mary owned a house a few blocks up the coast and they would gather every weekend to pick blue crabs of have fish or chowder together.

We laughed and talked a lot that night, but I noticed that Mother worked a long time at a small cup of the chowder. She said she felt full and couldn't eat much. This seemed to be happening more now, and we all could see how painfully thin she was becoming. Sometimes I wished she had been a heavier woman, wished she could have had more flesh to sustain her through the chemo, and the disease. It would give me more time with her—even another day.

Uncle Bob was oblivious, finishing his third bowl of chowder. He turned and pinched Mary's arm and joked as he always did, "Getting a little meaty there, aren't you Hon?" She smirked and retorted, "I'll diet tomorrow, thank you."

It was all such a predictable conversation, almost like a ritual, the casual good-natured teasing.

"Mary, never worry about a little weight," Mother said, breaking the pattern. "Never worry about that again."

There was nothing anyone could say.

Chapter Three

It was the end of August, Lew's birthday, when Mother called. Despite the weight loss and fatigue, she had been able to maintain her home, drive, and see a few friends. The summer had gone fairly well. I knew they were eating more fast food as Mother cooked less, and I had been making extra quantities when I prepared our meals so that I could take things down for them to freeze.

"I know it's Lew's birthday and I want to take you all out to dinner," Mother said.

I actually was looking forward to a quiet little celebration, just Lew and me, at the lake, but I agreed.

"Are you sure you feel like this?" I asked.

"Of course," came the reply.

"Okay," I said, "what time?"

When we arrived we entered through the back door onto the screened porch. I noticed that the flowers and window boxes, always a source of pride for my father, were withering and untended. The grass was trimmed, but weeds had begun to creep along the usually carefully edged walk in back. The bird feeder, customarily laden with seeds, was empty. Small things, I supposed. Lives in transition. There were more important concerns now.

Mother came onto the porch dressed in blue slacks and a creamy sweater. It was at least 75 degrees out, but she was cold. Even though I had seen her often I was shaken by how thin she had become. Maybe it was the dark slacks, or the way the light played on her face, but her cheekbones had become more prominent and when she smiled her lips looked thin and stretched, pulled across an unfamiliar expanse of teeth.

My God, I thought, so this is how it looks to starve.

I came in and hugged her, trying to stem my alarm, and was startled by the hard feel of bone.

"We're going to the steakhouse," she said, cheerily kissing my cheek. "Is that okay?"

"Sure," we said. Yet I had an odd feeling then of something uncomfortable in the air, a fey sense, like the way birds gather inland before a storm.

It was an odd evening, none of us able to quite find our footing, as if an alcoholic were in our midst, or as if something was unspoken, out of control. It was clear immediately that my father wouldn't walk or sit next to Mother. As we entered the restaurant he cleaved to Lew, leaving my mother trailing behind. I stood at the door, uncharacteristically holding it for her, and the two of us walked to a table together.

It was wrong. Father wanted a table off to the side of the restaurant. Rather than make an issue, we moved. When we were seated, he pulled his chair to a position awkwardly straddling a corner, as far as possible from Mother, as though his body space was somehow being invaded.

What was he thinking, I wondered? Did he believe cancer was contagious, like a common cold, like AIDS perhaps? I made a mental note to talk to him about this when we were alone. I couldn't understand it.

The steak was tough and Mother ate very little. She was trying bravely to keep up the conversation with questions about what we were doing at the lake, projects on the house. Lew answered and I was mostly quiet. Father talked a bit about the yard, about the dry weather and the difficulties of keeping the lawn watered. We finished dinner and then a small cake arrived with a single candle, ordered by Mother.

We sang a disharmonious "Happy Birthday" to Lew and congratulated him on his 40th.

I think we joked a bit about getting old. Lew said it was better than any of the alternatives—an old canard—then looked at his hands and seemed ashamed.

"Don't worry," Mother said quickly. "I'm not offended, Lew. It's just how life is, isn't it?" She paused, reflecting. "For a long time I asked 'why me? Why did this happen to me.' Then I thought, 'why not me?' "

I reached under the table and held her hand then and murmured something trivial about life being unfair, about injustice, then lied and said I thought she was doing better than anyone expected, that we could be hopeful that the chemo was making a difference. I didn't really believe it, but a phrase circled around my head, worthless maybe—something from Yeat's "rag and boneshop of the heart," and the need to make "ladders" in the midst of despair.

I pressed back the thought. We had some cake then. Again she ate little, said little. Sweets were becoming distasteful to her. Everything tasted too sweet.

Finally as we walked to the car, my father again separated himself from her, and again, I had the impression that he wanted to get away. And there was something else—something more—he was ashamed to be seen with her. She looked sick now, the thinness pronounced and clearly unhealthy. Yes, he seemed ashamed.

We got in the car, my father's car, like all the other new ones he got every two years, and rode to my parents' home incased in the polished, gleaming, perfect interior. When we reached the house, Lew, Mother, and Father went inside, but I was staring at the wall of the garage—the wall that held all the tools, my father's tools, lined up in stunning precision—each with its shape carefully outlined in marker on the wall. Nothing out of place. It was perfect, too perfect. And now his once-capable and attractive wife was no longer perfect.

My God, I asked silently, could this be?

***

Could it be? The words insinuated themselves in my head. Could it be? The question hung with a disquieting portent, casting a shadow over my mind.

I had always thought my mother was the perfectionist, that she was the one who always dressed me up in taffeta and gingham, braided my ponytails just so, insisted I always act with perfect decorum, be seen and not heard—unless, of course, it was on occasions when I was expected to perform.

And perform I did. I was a child with straight A's, the one beloved by teachers, singing solos in the school choir, winning scholarships, playing piano at all the recitals, making drawings and writing essays for the school paper. I was expected to do it all, and humbly, without fanfare or praise, for that could spoil the child.

The only time I felt the infinite fragility of my performance value was when I was 13 and failed to finish a piano accompaniment to a dress rehearsal of a fashion show at the local Women's Club. The piano pedal was broken and my notes sounded puny and disconnected; I could not finish the composition. It was only a rehearsal after all, but the other mothers were there, including the prominent women married to doctors or from families we did not associate with.

My mother pulled me into the lobby, shook my shoulders and seethed with rage. "Don't ever embarrass me that way again," she threatened between clenched teeth. "Not ever again."

I didn't. It was about her, after all, not me.

The message was conveyed: perform.

I had to perform for her, achieve for her. And if I failed to do as I was told, or later as a teenager to follow her fundamental moral compass, I would be roundly criticized, slapped, or spanked.

Being a child, I thought this was normal, that all children were sometimes kicked around for "talking back" or behaving "improperly." It was my inferior position to be treated this way, I thought, and it was only years later in college that I realized I was wrong.

It was also the case that in most noisily confrontational arguments between my parents, I would be asked to take sides. This virtually assured that the argument would inevitably shift its focus to me. Through it all, although my father clenched his fist and threatened and his loud anger terrified me, it was my mother who physically punished.

It was a paradox, and a dilemma, because I always felt so protective of her, confided in her, and always gave her the emotional support she rarely received from my father. As an only child, I wordlessly intuited that I was the glue at the center of my parents' world, the thing that held it all together, and though my mother sometimes talked of divorce, she never followed through.

Other memories went through my mind, resurrected briefly. I had laid them aside I thought, slathered them over with the hundreds of encouraging and wonderful times that my mother had been there for me, had sacrificed for me, had attended all my school programs, award ceremonies, and piano recitals where my father had seldom appeared. But now I saw the kaleidoscope shifting and moments of wounding flashing like segments of a silent film.

I saw the perfect house, the floors scrubbed and gleaming, the sofa that no dog, no pet, no animal, was ever allowed to violate. And there was me, the wild daughter who ran home from school to play war games with the neighbor boy, who slithered through the tall green field of rye that stretched to the old railroad tracks, and who climbed too high into the brittle limbs of the apple trees. I was the dirty one who crawled into the wooden barrel filled with straw to sleep with the dog, and who lived on the beach in the summertime, rescuing starfish and minnows and muddy horseshoe crabs trapped in tidepools.

I supposed it was my parents' misfortune that I was all of these things, and that I became a blue-jeaned, tie-dyed hippie, at least in their eyes, one of those ungrateful college revolutionaries who believed the political system was despicable. I was anti-war and pro civil rights, against all their conservative judgments, and I challenged every certitude they passionately held dear. Yet I think they both gave up after awhile, and as incongruous as it may seem, I never doubted that they loved me in all their argumentative and confusing fervor.

We were just different, but our love was fierce. I shuddered to think what my emotional life would have been like had my mother not survived her cancer many years ago, or had my father not been there with his steadfast work ethic, or his gift for song and humor. They had nurtured me, worked hard, and put me through college, loved and accepted Lew, and been the steady platform from which I had launched my life.

Now I saw that platform collapsing. They were struggling and the old patterns were shifting. And we were all passing through something cavernous and overwhelming. I wanted to help them, grieved for them, hoped for them, and again—I was dismayed at the behavior of my father.

As I had done so often in the past, I sought the refuge of forgetfulness in canvas, in mediums and pigments, in creation of the small kingdom that I alone controlled. I sought the solace of my studio and remained there till I could again face the turmoil of the world around me.

***

It is a little known principle in painting, in observation, that in order to see the small reflected highlight on the shadow edge of a round object, you need to focus your eyes on another point in the composition. You need to look away.

In the beginning of September I was trying to do that. I was painting the lily pond on our property, the weathered barn of our neighbor, the muted sunsets across the mirroring lake—and I was looking away. I was painting anything that would divert my thoughts. I was trying not to focus on the details of the larger composition into which my life had irretrievably been descending.

"When will you be starting classes?" my students were calling to ask.

"Not till the beginning of October this year," I replied. "I have some painting projects to finish. And you know my mother is ill and I want to spend some time with her."

They understood. Most of them had been with me a long time and I was grateful for their loyalty.

Usually when I stopped at the house now, Mother was on the sofa in the sunroom. She said she would be up awhile, but then just felt that she "had to get down." In the times when she was "up" she would talk to friends who stopped by, or perhaps do some errands or simple chores. Yet I could see the house was looking different.....not neglected....but sterile. There were no informal little bouquets of garden flowers around the rooms, no smells of sugar cookies or muffins in the kitchen, no evidence of the gentle beauty with which she had always filled these walls.

"I just wish I could go to the shore again," she said, laying there, arm over her forehead. "I just feel like I'd like to wade in the ocean again."

I looked at the cards from well-meaning friends on the table...all depressing in the cheerily irritable and superficial sameness of their messages, the African violet struggling to hold onto its remaining leaves, the trees in the yard just preternaturally edged in brown after the dry heat of summer. My father had the sprinkler going and was putting some gardening equipment in the shed outside. The world, I thought, *her* world, is narrowing, so little to look forward to. I guess that's why I suggested it.

"Well, why don't we do it? September is a beautiful month, and all the crowds are gone from the shore. It will be like old times again with us at Sea Isle."

"But, could you do that?" she asked, turning on the sofa.

"Could you leave Lew? And what about your classes?"

"Mother," I said sarcastically, "Lew's a big boy. He can take care of himself quite well, and I don't start classes till October. We should go down tomorrow and look at some places."

"Yes?" she said, smiling and working over the thought.

The next day we left for the shore, visiting realtors and checking out rentals. After looking at only two places I could see this was all exhausting and wearing on her, and she left the remainder of the inspections to me. I hastily settled on a simple downstairs apartment in the same neighborhood as our old summer cottage. The house backed up against a dune where wild bayberry and morning glories thrived amid the beach grasses. It was modestly furnished but had east facing windows that caught sea breezes in the afternoons. I returned to the realtor and left a deposit for the third week in September.

***

We came to the coast when the days were warm but with just a hint of fall in the air. The beach was nearly deserted, a grand expanse spotted with random sandbars and glistening tidepools. The water was still comfortable and inviting, and our days were spent in its presence, walking, wading, or sitting beside the sea.

At night from our small porch we could see the constellations in their radiant clarity bending to Earth, comets falling to the edge of the horizon, blending with the glow of distant freighters or the insignificant flickerings of lights along the shore.

This part of the Atlantic coast was still spare, still unrecovered from the storms of the 60's that washed most of the old summer cottages away. It was however saved; saved for the seabirds and dune grasses, the red-winged blackbirds and herring gulls, and too, it seemed, for us.

We spent the week alone. Lew was working at his teaching job and could only come in the evenings. My father did not want to join us. As it was, both came only occasionally to take their meals with us. It was just as well. My father seemed content to be home, and he viewed me as something of a nurse, relieving him of a presumed burden.

I couldn't, again, look at it. I focused my eyes away and determined to make this instead a time that Mother and I could remember.

In the manner that routines are rediscovered after many years, we settled into an old familiar beach life. We rose each morning and took a slow walk along the glassy shore, our eyes adjusted for the remarkable shell or the glistening gem-like stone, alert for the beached jellyfish or scurrying sand crab. We always returned with a bucket of treasures which we piled on the back step, near the hose where we washed sand from our feet.

In the afternoons, Mother sat on her beach chair, writing letters or postcards at the edge of the sea, or sometimes napped on the sofa at the cottage. Enjoué was usually beside her, watchful and affectionate.

That week we did things without forethought or planning. We went to the boardwalk and bought gifts for the neighborhood children, made gaudy necklaces of puka shells, and purchased boxes of Copper Kettle fudge that no one ever ate. We had tea at bayside piers, waded in the ocean, and made spaghetti sauce using the bay leaves Mother gathered from the dune. We gently walked, created, and talked our way through the days. And sometime in late-week, when a cold front came through, I think we saw a miracle.

***

It came in the night with the wind, with the erratic and restless wind that precedes a front, a change. I rose to close windows and felt the house shudder slightly. The windows were jammed with the swelling of the summer, and I took a book and pounded them down, waking Mother. We were up then, and pulled on sweaters over our nightgowns. It was still dark and too early to eat breakfast.

"Want to see the sunrise?" I asked.

Outside it was quiet and tenebrous, with just a faint suggestion of light to the east. The coolness accompanied us as we crossed the dune, the change that the front had brought apparent in the chill air and feel of the sand under our feet. We descended to the beach below, following the strip of gray light unfolding out along the coast. The waves made a sibilate hissing sound as we walked, a chorus of tiny bubbles forming and breaking into ribbons of salty foam. The sea was stirring from the passing winds, disengaging itself in long white breakers after the tumult of the night. Curving up the beach I could barely discern a line of dark debris, bits of broken life disgorged and abandoned on the shore. We walked along, stooping to return to the sea some stranded conches and crustaceans nearly buried in mounds of seaweed.

I don't know how long we proceeded this way, but at some point we became aware the dim twilight around us was subtly lifting. We stopped then and watched as far off, along the horizon, a touch of pink began reaching toward the base of the distant clouds. An upper ridge of cumulous gradually took up the rose, transferring and amplifying it across the eastern sky. Near the horizon a few long tendrils of light reached into the upper air, rays that emanated from somewhere below our line of sight. From a place we could not see, the light was reaching to dispel the darkness. There was a moment of stillness, a breath, as if the very molecules of air were waiting patiently to receive the light. Then suddenly the horizon split apart and the sun flashed above the sea, disintegrating the rose into a prism of color, sending orange and gold strobing the waves, casting deep shadows on the dunes and grasses, and tearing open the September sky.

We both stood transfixed.

"I've never seen a sunrise as beautiful as this, Belva Ann," she said, touching my hand.

Neither had I.

We stood there a long time as the waves flicked rosy sea smoke in their curls and till the first gulls drifted in from the marshes to greet the sun. And I believe it was there, on a deserted beach, despite the sorrow within and around us, that I understood the joy of being fully present to the moment. I learned that on a beach, under a sunrise, with my mother.

Chapter Four

It was an early autumn that year. In mid-October the leaves began to turn, the swamp maples picking up touches of vermillion and burgundy, the aspens and sycamores devolving into canopies of tarnished golds.

I admired the changeling trees as I drove to my parents' house, was diverted from my usual worry about them by the beauty of nature around me. But when I arrived I found Mother crying on the sofa. She was restless and distressed. My father, she said, wouldn't take her anywhere.

"Why won't he take you out?" I asked, as uncertain as she was.

"I don't know. He just says I need to lie down. I wanted to go for a drive to see the fall colors—you know how I always love the fall—but he won't do it. He won't take me anywhere."

I looked out the window to see my father with his leaf-catcher, going in circles on the perfect grass. It struck me as a profligately despicable image.

"I'll take you out," I blurted. "Where would you like to go?"

"Could you take me to Carmel?" she said, wiping her eyes. "The trees are always so pretty along the road there."

I got her a sweater from the bedroom and we left. I saw again how emaciated she was, yet she walked easily to the car and seemed alert and eager for the little excursion. I wondered what was wrong with my father, what was the skewered sense of priorities that enabled him to place a patch of meaningless grass above the dwindling moments of joy he might give to his wife? What character flaw or act of aversion could explain a behavior that seemed so inexcusable?

I pushed these thoughts away that day and focused on the drive. Like our lives, so much had changed here since I was a kid. A new college had grown in the woods where I once walked. The narrow road to Carmel had been repaved with an improved bridge over a small upper tributary of the Maurice River. I had canoed here, and swum along its tangled banks with Lew. As we came upon it again, the trees picked up a tapestry of color, the purples, oranges, and peach tones repeating on the stream in a hundred mirrored subtleties of color.

"Can you stop here?" Mother asked, taken with the magnificence of the scene.

I pulled off the road and we sat looking at the woodlands, the windows rolled down to admit the sound of tinkling water, passing over deadfalls, rushing along the clotted banks. From somewhere in the forest a small branch snapped.

"I don't think I'll see fall again," she said. "I know I'm failing, Belva Ann."

It was said so simply, so unemotionally, merely with a breath of longing in her voice, a melancholy as though she were letting the wonder of the world ebb away.

Everything I'd been holding in, everything I had constricted inside, every sorrow I had known congregated in an instant to that place.

My head fell on the wheel and I sobbed.

"Oh, honey, I'm so sorry, I didn't want to make you sad," she said.

"I love you so much. How could I not be sad?" I asked through a blur of tears.

We held each other as the stream continued its murmurings, as the trees wavered in their golden light, and as the world passed on the highway, unconcerned.

"It's okay," she said, "I'm okay. Whatever happens, I'm at

peace with it. I just don't want you to be sad for too long. You have your whole life ahead of you. I've lived mine."

I blew my nose and shook my head in protest.

"No, stop," she said. "It's a beautiful day and I don't want to spoil it. Take me to Carmel. I want to stop at the little fruit stand there and get some pumpkins."

She was always so good at pulling my heart strings, then changing the subject back to the mundane—a practical woman, unaccustomed to long contemplation, compassionate from her early losses but not wallowing in grief. Her life was like that, doing what needed to be done, responsible, accepting the reality of what is.

She had worked as a telephone operator before she met my father, and when I was born she became absorbed in the role of wife and mother. Later, when I was 13, she began taking college classes and gradually earned enough credits to be hired in a new area of teaching: special education. There she continued for 15 years, soon bringing in a bigger salary than my father who had a job then in the glass industry. It was a source of conflict, a hard transition, and I don't believe they ever bridged the resentment that the disparate earning power created. Yet her efforts enabled me, in part, to go to college while she worked two jobs, that of managing a household, and as teacher to the mentally challenged.

The families of her students loved her. The children called her "Missus Penn." She mentored all of them with understanding and concern. She accepted their struggles and handicaps at a time when understanding of the disabled was in short supply. I think she grew as a person then, and in ways I had not always seen in my childhood.

And we spoke of this as we drove to Carmel. We spoke of her teaching days there in the small brick schoolhouse. We circled the old dirt playground and looked in windows at the classrooms, no longer used. I had visited there on vacations from college, and I knew the voices and the faces of the children she had helped. The notes from their grateful families still came on holidays, their affection apparent in expressions of concern for her now.

On the way back we stopped at the fruit stand where we both bought some bright orange pumpkins and Indian corn.

"I'm going to put a face on this one," she said, holding it for me to see. "I'll use a magic marker and your father can put it out on the front porch. The kids should like it."

It was a modest gourd and I carried it to the car, wondering if my father would even be willing to perform this small task. I was worried about both of them now, but I also was trying to take things one day at a time. I was glad we had this afternoon together and tried not to think of the rest.

***

Sometimes you see things coming, but very slowly. You see out of some peripheral vision, out of the corner of your eye, as if a shadow has passed, but you can't quite mark its passage, or the time when everything changed. I felt I was moving in an indeterminate current like that, small changes, small decisions, actions flowing out of reactions, out of needs, but the larger journey eluding me. Yet I felt I had slipped into a truly foreign realm when I came to the house that day and heard my father yelling at my mother. I could barely make out the words, but there was frustration and anger in them.

Mother was on the sofa and he was standing over her.

"I don't know what the bollix you want, Belva," he was saying loudly.

She mumbled something indiscernible as I walked in. Then he turned angrily to me, almost as if he expected me to be there..

"I don't know what she wants. She's not making any sense."

I looked at her as she lay there, waving her hand helplessly over her face. I dropped onto the edge of the sofa.

"What's wrong, Mommy? What is it?"

She babbled something incoherent, seeming frustrated that she could not form the words. I grabbed her shoulders, looking at her intently. "Try again," I said slowly.

She tried, but it was useless, and in some way I felt she knew this was so.

"You know what you want to say, don't you?" I asked. She nodded her head. "But you just can't say it?" Again, a nod of relief at being understood.

"Are you in pain?" I asked. She shook her head, no.

"Okay. I'm going to call the doctor and we'll see what to do. You try to be still. I'll be right back." She looked away and I could see the fear in her eyes then.

I ran to the kitchen, trembling, and fumbled for the number of the oncologist. His receptionist miraculously answered and put me right through.

"It sounds like a TIA," he said, after I blurted and stumbled out a description of what was happening. "It's a transient ischemic attack, like a little stroke , and we see it sometimes in cancer patients or in older people as they get frailer and have circulatory problems. Just watch her for a few minutes, and if she doesn't come out of it, or if it gets worse, bring her immediately to the ER. I can meet you there."

I hung up and was turning toward the porch when Father stopped me.

"I don't know what she wants. She doesn't make any sense. She's not right. Your mother's crazy." He was more agitated, more irritated, than I'd seen him in a long time.

"Daddy," I whispered, exasperated, "She's *not* crazy. She may be having a little stroke—something the doctor calls a TIA. We need to be calm and see if she comes out of it—AND it doesn't help with you yelling at her for something that is not her fault!"

He was breathing rapidly and seemed disgusted, and perhaps offended. I couldn't deal with it then and left him to stew while I went back to Mother.

"Are you feeling any better?" I asked, not really expecting an answer.

"Uh-hum," she said.

I felt a wave of relief.

"Can you tell me what happened?"

She began to form a few words—"I, I couldn't—seem—to eat anything—right."

"You couldn't eat?"

She shook her head, trying again,"I couldn't *say* it right."

"Listen, Mommy. This will pass. The doctor says you should be okay in a few minutes. Do you understand?"

She nodded her head.

I stayed with her for the remainder of the afternoon, then called a nurse who was a friend of the family. She gave some confirmation about what the doctor had described. We would merely be vigilant for now.

But this was not acceptable to my father. "Your mother should be in a hospital—or a nursing home," he said.

"Daddy, I told you what the doctor said. We just need to be watchful. These things can happen sometimes, but she should come out of it fairly quickly."

"No, she shouldn't be here. She needs to be in a home." He was resuming his litany.

I looked about the house. It was picked up, there was food in the refrigerator, and a freezer full of meals I had sent down or neighbors had brought to them. Mother still cared for herself, as well as handling all the bills and finances. I knew Daddy was doing more errands and grocery shopping, but Mother seemed able to manage the rest.

"I can't take care of her," he said again, following me around. "She needs a nurse."

"Why? Do you have to cook for her?" I asked.

"No."

"Bathe her, dress her, do her laundry?"

"No...but she's not herself."

"Do you have to give her medicines, take her phone calls,

help her walk, things like that?"

"No, no, but she's not right!" he protested.

"You mean she's *not right for you!*" I shot back angrily.

He looked stricken, like he'd been slapped. He was always uncomfortable with illness—with disease. Dis-ease. He avoided the sick, hospital visits unless under duress, even funerals. He especially was uncomfortable with people he thought of as crazy, as though this might be a choice, or a character flaw. I always wondered if there was some mental illness in the family, maybe with his uncle, the one he knew as a boy and nicknamed Pennio, who lived as a hermit in a shack on Union Lake. It seemed this person had troubled him greatly.

I couldn't know, and at any rate, I didn't care. At that moment I simply thought his desire to put Mother away while she was still able to have something of a life was despicable.

"Look, Daddy," I said, lowering my tone. "I'll see about getting you some help, possibly a home health aide a few days a week, and a visiting nurse to check on Mother. But you have to let me know if she has any more of these episodes of not being able to speak—and DON'T yell at her. She can't help what's happening."

I could see he was not satisfied, but there was nothing else at the time that I could think to do. If he was this incapable now, I wondered, what would he do when things got really bad? I looked at him hard, and prepared myself for the possibility that Mother might need to come live with me.

***

"We're having a wonderful time in Hawaii," the postcard read. The writer described the views of the stunning mountains, the incredible fun of traveling on such a remote island of the world. It was from close friends of my parents.

I wondered if they realized, even with a small measure of awareness, that people confronting illness, navigating from one crisis to the next, grappling with the awesome finalities of life, might not be so disposed to hear of the resplendent adventures of others. Such would probably not occur to them. And I guessed these communications were merely aspects of their narcissism, or of a culture which chooses to ignore illness and death.

Instead of support, Mother was often treated to interminable visits and phone calls from people who superficially prattled on about their lives, avoiding the very large unpleasant elephant in the room. While few were able to hear her with real compassion, she was expected to listen to the plans of others—from the exalted to the mundane—and all while dealing with fatigue and illness. This was what our society often calls "tending the sick," and I found it appalling.

Mother didn't confront the issue directly, but she was beginning to ask my father, or the health aide, to field her calls. The phone rang constantly, mostly calls from people who were only remotely connected to my parents, and so we disconnected it in her room so she could rest. It wasn't that she resented seeing close friends; it was just that the visits were often unscheduled and overlong. She was also feeling the need to get away, and one of her acquaintances suggested she and my father go to a nice quiet seaside hotel in Ocean City for the weekend.

I knew Father probably wouldn't want to go, but it was only for two days, and I offered to ride down with them on a Friday to help them get settled in. Lew was going to join us after school and we planned to all have a light supper together in the hotel dining room. Mother had reserved a suite of rooms oceanside and was looking forward to the change of scene.

"You really think your mother's up to this?" my father said when I entered the house that day of the little trip.

He was looking ill at ease and I wasn't sure he was even going.

"Yes. She's up to it. The doctor said she should do as

much as she feels she can do. I think this will do you both some good—to get away for a couple of days. And you can do what you want—order room service, enjoy the view, watch some movies..."

He said nothing...then, "Me pants don't look good."

"Oh, Daddy, your pants are fine." *Here we go again,* I thought.

"Well, I've got to find some better pants. See how much weight I've lost?" He stood up and did another pull-the-waistband-and-expose-the-gap-of-flesh-and-fabric-routine.

I had to admit he had lost some weight, yet I knew he felt better than he had in years after seeing the cardiologist and getting new medication. I assumed he was worrying some of the weight off. The anxiety was hard on everyone.

"You look nice, Daddy. When you get back I'll take your measurements and we'll go get you some new clothes, but for now, you really look fine."

Mother came out then, looking like she'd put some thought into her outfit, wearing a nice blue jacket, matching slacks, and a paisley scarf. The clothes were loose on her, but then, everything was now.

I don't remember what was said on the drive down—the usual small talk I presume. When we got to Ocean City we saw the impressive height of the new hotel dominating the modest skyline. It rose over what had once been a coastal dune at the southern end of the island. A small nature preserve extended out to the inlet, and newer homes had sprung up around the hotel. Father turned into a wide parking area and slowed the car, oddly looking back at me.

"You're really going to do this to us, aren't you?" he said.

"What?" I asked, startled.

"You're really going to leave us here. You're going to put us away."

"John....," Mother said, "we're at the hotel. Belva Ann's going to stay and have dinner with us. What did you think she was going to do?"

He didn't answer. We were stopped under the portico by the entrance where I had gotten out and was holding the car door for Mother. She had one foot on the sidewalk, the rest of her body still in the car, when my father said, "I ain't gonna do it. You're not gonna put us here!"

He slammed his foot on the gas as my mother screamed, half in, half out of the moving car. I saw them careen away, squealing across the parking lot, but I couldn't take my eye off her foot, the one dragging on the asphalt, with her begging for him to stop.

I ran, screaming then too, chasing the car, terrified Mother would lose her grip on the door, fall or be pulled under the wheel.

Finally I saw the car slow and pause as Mother barely got out, staggering. The passenger door was still open as my father sped away.

She was there alone in the middle of an empty parking lot. I ran up to her and grabbed her. We were both so shaken that neither of us could speak till we caught our breath.

"Are you hurt?" I panted, terrified.

"No, I'm okay. My ankle turned a little I think."

"Can you walk on it?" I asked.

"I think so," she said in a shaking voice.

"Good. Just lean on me and we'll go inside and sit down in the lobby."

What had happened was so unthinkable, so unimaginable. I suppose we were both in a kind of physical shock.

"Do you think he'll come back?" she asked as we sat in a corner of the lobby, me examining her ankle, she clutching her handbag and rubbing a hand over her leg.

"I don't know....but I do know that he almost killed you."

"Where do you think he could have gone?" she asked.

It was rhetorical. "I haven't a clue, Mother, and at this point I'm not sure I much care. He's only thinking of himself anyway." The shock was wearing off and rage was replacing it.

I looked at her ankles, both somewhat swollen with edema, and saw again her fragile right foot being dragged along the parking lot, the shoe nearly falling off, her hand clutching the open door.....I shut my eyes to block it out.

"We have no car," I said, "no bags, nothing. We might as well go up to the room. It's paid for. We can at least wait awhile in comfort."

"Yes. Maybe he'll come back," Mother said.

And so we waited all afternoon, looking at the ocean, ordering some sandwiches from room service, and waiting some more. I called Father's cousin Ed and his wife Joan who lived in Ocean City, and explained what had happened. They appeared within a half hour and talked to us, good sounding boards who validated our decision that Father needed emotional help. Late in the day, Lew appeared and heard the whole story again.

"What do you want to do? he asked. "Shall I take you home now?"

There was no point in staying. Father was not going to reappear. The much-awaited weekend was over before it began, and now there was another crisis to deal with.

"Yes," said Mother. "Maybe he's back at the house."

"If not," I said, "we should call the police. There's no telling what he might do."

***

"It was getting dark as we pulled into the driveway. Through the glare of the headlights I could see the silver Camry in the garage. Lights were on in the living room, but the door was locked. We pressed the buzzer and my father peered suspiciously through a slit in the curtains, then silently opened the door. I noted he was breathing heavily and looked either frightened or ashamed.

"Where did you go, John? Why did you leave me like that?" Mother asked. She was far kinder and more understanding with her introductory questions than I would have been.

He darted his eyes around like he was trying to figure it out, like something didn't quite align in his mind. "I wasn't going to be put away....not in no home," he blurted.

"You think the hotel was a nursing home?" I asked, amazed.

He looked at me like I was lying.

"I just surmised that you were gonna leave us there, your mother and me."

"John," Mother said, "where in the world would you get a crazy notion like that?"

"Well, I just surmised they could get rid of both of us."

"Who is 'they'? Mother asked. "Your daughter? Lew?...Oh John..." she groaned and slumped into a chair.

"Is that what you think, Daddy? Is that what you think of me, that I would do that?"

He raised his voice angrily. "I just know that something's not right, that I haven't felt welcome at your house for a long time." His sudden anger frightened me, and at that moment I knew we couldn't leave Mother alone with him.

"Lew," I said. "You stay with Daddy while I help Mother put a few of her things in the car. She's coming with us."

As I gathered up some extra clothes and toiletries and stuffed them into Mother's already packed suitcase my mind reeled with images of his behavior over the past years. He was, in part, right. I had been angry with him, some part of me had harbored resentment for his apparent lack of interest in my life. I knew my father had always wanted a son. Indeed, he had been there for countless games of horseshoes and badminton, all the "boy things" in the back yard where he taught me how to throw my first curve ball, or ride a two wheel bike. He had taken me to gather teaberries in the woods, and had shown me how to fish and steer his many boats. I treasured these times, but as for my creative life, he expressed utter disinterest. He rarely came into my studio, and then only to praise Lew's carpentry work while my paintings sat on easels, forlornly ignored. He refused to attend most of my piano recitals and art shows, saying he didn't want to be around all those "big Muckety-Mucks." I felt that since my childhood, it was Mother who had always made an effort to be there for me. It only seemed my father's disinterested behavior had gotten worse with age as he became more and more withdrawn—and now it seemed to be too much trouble to be there for Mother too.

As I crossed the living room with a suitcase in hand I told him I'd be back tomorrow and we would talk about finding him a therapist, someone to talk to. I was irate. "You're not seeing things clearly, not thinking clearly. And I'm afraid you're a danger to Mother. I'll be back tomorrow."

"I haven't eaten," he countered.

"What? You've got a ton of food in the refrigerator. Go heat yourself something," I shot back.

I couldn't believe it—he was sitting in the chair, looking upset that no one was going to make him dinner after he'd just put us through a day of hell.

"Well, I'm not staying here," he suddenly announced, shooting up, grabbing his car keys, and heading toward the garage.

We all looked at each other, momentarily immobile, till we heard the automatic garage door grumbling open and a car door sharply close.

"I'll go stop him," I gasped, arriving just in time to see him starting the engine, preparing, I supposed, another flight.

I opened the passenger door. "Daddy, don't!" I said as authoritatively as I could with a hoarse voice. "You don't want to go anywhere. Not now." But he was already locked in reverse, backing toward the exit, and I suddenly felt slammed by the open door against my hip and arm. I was being swept backward.

The garage was a nightmare of sharp gardening tools, with only a few inches between the wall and the open car door. Behind me I sensed the corner of the garage looming up and instantly felt the prickling panic of being crushed against its cinder block hardness. I was screaming, being dragged.

Then Mother suddenly appeared in the doorway and I heard her scream over my own. Father stopped and she stumbled toward me. My back was mere inches from the wall. "You could have killed Belva Ann!" she kept screaming. "You could have killed Belva Ann!" She was pounding a frail fist on the hood of the Camry, tears flowing down her wasted cheeks. I closed the car door and Father rocketed out of the garage, brakes squealing as he turned up the street and disappeared into the night.

Chapter Five

The police found him sitting in his car on the side of the road, looking dazed, and he passively came with them after our night of worry. The whole episode seemed to have chastened him. The police wanted him now, he thought, and he was obedient, submissive, and on good behavior.

We were in the psychiatrist's office the next day, my father and I, and surprisingly it had not taken much persuasion to get him there.

"Why do you think you're here?" the psychiatrist asked my father.

He looked rumpled and wary. "Well....I know I've been having some problems with my wardrobe."

I almost laughed, but stopped when I looked at his serious face and realized how earnest he was.

"Your wardrobe?" the doctor asked.

"Yes. It's me pants. I don't have nothin' to wear that fits me...and I've lost weight."

I suppressed a groan.

The doctor looked across the table at me, then wrote some notes on a pad.

"You think you're here because of your clothes?"

"Well...I guess so." Then as a secondary thought, "I know my wife's sick and she needs to be in a hospital...and my daughter says I need to talk to you." He looked at me again then, suspicious.

The conversation made little sense, and after an hour of confusion I was glad I had given the doctor a description of what was occurring before he saw my father.

"I think you're very depressed," he said finally, "but I think we can help you."

Then he pulled me aside as a nurse examined Father and took his vital signs. "There's a lot of paranoia and delusion here. Usually with patients this disturbed we require some intensive medical intervention to begin to pull them out. I would suggest hospitalization."

How long?" I asked.

"At least a month, maybe longer," he replied.

"My mother may be gone by then. Is there really no other way?" I whispered.

"No...I really think this is best."

When my father was seated again, the doctor asked, "Are you willing to go for some help, Mr. Penn?"

My father looked at me expressionlessly, then nodded.

It was all so simple. There was amazingly no protest. My father signed some papers giving permission for his treatment, his beautiful handwriting now shaky and deliberative, and we went home to gather up a few of his belongings. He packed the new pants and two new flannel shirts I had bought him and chattered as if he were going on a vacation. He was leaving his home of many years, yet I felt he wanted to go. Whatever fears of being "put away" had haunted him, they now seemed to have dissolved in the actual fact as mysteriously as they arose.

He checked the basement then went out into the yard and filled the bird feeder for the last time, throwing a handful of seeds on the ground for Pete the Squirrel, then we locked the door and left. Lew and I drove him to the hospital that evening and watched as some nurses gently led him down the hall. He was carrying his old suitcase and he looked small and hunched as he turned into a room and the door softly closed.

My heart ached, hurt in a way that seemed inconceivable only a few months before. My family was fracturing, cast about in ways I never thought possible. I didn't even know my father anymore, who he was, or what he had become. When we went back to the lake, Lew and I, I tried to put a positive face on it all for Mother.

"He needs help. He's not himself. I know he will at least have a chance of getting help there," I said to her. "And we'll be able to see him often, after the first week or so."

"Yes," she said. "I know it has to be. I just hope your father can pull himself together. I don't know what will become of him."

She was worried, deeply worried for him. I wondered how she did it, how she held herself together despite everything. I admired her strength then. We would, I felt, all have need of it.

***

In late October Mother settled into a guest room with a view facing west over the lake. It had a Victorian brass bed with a patchwork quilt, an ornate if non-functional little chimney stove, a small oak desk and some padded wicker chairs. I was glad I had stripped the wallpaper and painted it the year before. Little did I know I would be needing it so soon.

In the afternoons the sun on the lake made hundreds of tiny dancing refracted lights on the walls, giving the room the appearance of being ashimmer in floating crystals.

Usually Mother came down for a small brunch of tea, orange juice and toast, then would lie on the sofa in the living room, sometimes reading, sometimes napping. Occasionally three or four of my older students that were part of her acquaintance would stop in after a class to say hello. I was demoted then from teacher to the role of hostess.

"Belva Ann, make some tea...or maybe you would all like coffee? And don't we have at least some cookies or a cake? We should have something to give you." She was forever trying to feed her company, and I was usually tired and paint-stained and definitely not a baker. I complied as best I could while she chatted with some amazing reserve of newfound energy, always gracious to everyone. I knew these visits gave her some small interaction and connection with the world. Her women friends too were loyal and sometimes stopped with books or food, and once in awhile she would sit on the dock with them if the weather was warm enough.

But she was never able to visit my father. By evening, the time of hospital visiting hours, she was simply too tired. Lew then assumed the responsibility of looking in on him, and he did this nearly every day. Somehow, we all seemed to manage. Through it all I don't recall a time that Mother was difficult, or angry, or complaining. She knew that we were doing all we could. She would ask about Father, but I did not tell her everything. It was too troubling.

***

I suppose it was the medication, the effort to find a balance between controlling the anxiety without over-medicating the patient. It may have been the unfamiliarity of the place itself, the way the sterility and strangeness of it induced a kind of lethargy. I could not know. I only was aware that the first weeks of my father's hospitalization were a time in which he descended into a delusional and near unconscious state.

"What are you giving him?" I asked the staff. "He's looking and acting like a zombie. This can't be helping him."

"No," said a nurse. "This is typical. Here's what the doctor prescribed. Once he gets used to it, once his body adjusts, he'll begin to be more responsive."

I didn't understand it. And I had scant confidence in medicine or psychotherapy then, but there was no alternative. At times his unresponsiveness bordered on catatonia, and after a few minutes I would simply leave.

I think it was sometime around his third week at the hospital that he became more animated. I saw him one evening, sitting in his room, talking with his roommate, a thin middle-aged man whom my father introduced as Tom. He and Tom had been in group therapy together and it seemed they had developed a relationship.

"Well, it's good to see you up, Daddy," I said, smiling.

"Yes," he replied, "I'm just starting to learn the ropes around here. This is a hospital, isn't it?"

"Yes, Daddy. How are you doing? Is everything okay? Are they treating you okay?"

"Oh yeh...they all stick their heads in the door and ask how you're doin', then they leave." he said.

"And how's the food?"

"It's all right—not like you or your mother's cookin', but then I've not got much of an appetite, so it doesn't matter I guess."

"Can I get you anything?"

"Well, I could use another sweater...the brown one with the two pockets. It gets cold here at night....and I could use me thicker socks too."

"Sure, I'll get them for you when I come again."

"And how's your mother?" he suddenly asked.

"Mommy's doing okay. Of course she misses you," I said.

"She's still sick?" he asked implausibly.

"Yes."

He looked out at the empty hallway, thinking, speaking almost absently. "I just figured that when I come home this'll all be over."

"You mean...that Mother will be gone?" I asked, feeling a little lurch in my stomach.

He nodded.

I looked at him, and perhaps it was my own sense of fatigue at trying to hold everything together, dealing with this alone, but I believed that he *wanted* it to be over, *wanted* to be out of it, *wanted* to remove himself till all this unpleasantness had passed. Well...you've gotten what you wanted, I thought to myself.

I sat on the bed with him and we said little till visiting hours were over.

"I'll tell Mother you were asking about her. Lew will be here tomorrow and I'll have him bring your sweater and socks. I gave him a hug which he limply returned, and I left.

***

I don't remember exactly when it happened again, but it came suddenly, without warning, the next TIA. Mother was eating at the table, putting sugar on her potatoes, reaching for the salt and pepper for her coffee, unsure of which utensil to use, her movements irrational and uncoordinated. She couldn't speak, and this time she seemed utterly uncomprehending.

The oncologist insisted I bring her immediately to the Emergency Room. The nurses there quickly took over, putting in an IV, rushing her out of sight. I waited outside, feeling helpless. An hour later, when I could join her in the ER, her communication skills had improved and she showed no signs of any paralysis—just some mild confusion about what had happened.

As I talked to her, holding her hand, she said that she wanted to go home, but the ER doctors insisted she stay overnight "for observation." I reluctantly left after she got settled into a room, promising to return first thing in the morning.

I found her the next day sitting up on the edge of the bed and begging to go home. I ran to her and hugged her tightly.

"The doctors want me to have some tests," she said. "I don't want any more."

"What kind of tests?" I asked.

"Oh, I don't know...some kinds of scans."

I looked at her sallow face, the emaciated body with the

swollen feet barely able to wedge into their loose slippers, and I wondered what could be gained by subjecting her to more tests and probing.

I put my arm around her shrunken shoulders and wanted to hold her till the Universe fell around us and the planets collided in their tragic orbits and we could throw our souls into the blackness and defy this terrible disease that was upon us. Instead I said, "Let me see if I can talk to the doctor. I don't think you should spend another day in this place unless it's absolutely necessary. I'm going to the nurses' station to find out when the doctor makes his rounds."

I felt like her defender, *was* her defender, her protector. I didn't like the hospital, didn't like the noise, didn't like her room. It was all gray and cheerless. How many days did she have left, I wondered? And why should she spend a single one looking at the façade of an ugly concrete building from a wretched hospital window?

"We need to see if the cancer has spread to the brain," her doctor said when I finally tracked him down.

"Why do you need to know?" I asked.

He looked at me like I had just challenged some established law of physics, a given of nature, like gravity.

"Well...so we can understand the course of the disease. She may become paralyzed, have a larger stroke. We don't know what we're dealing with."

"Doctor," I drew out the opening, "she has, maybe, six months to live, and she's lived five of them." I waited, studying his face. "What is the point? Could you operate if you knew? Change her treatment? Deal better with pain? What is the benefit?" I looked for an answer, but he simply seemed to be studying Mother's charts, a visual graph of decline, while he tried, I guessed, to come up with some compelling justifications.

I thought then that medicine was too often about acquiring information rather than comforting or helping the sick. Defensive medicine. The threat of lawsuits. I tried to continue...

"My mother knows her prognosis, doctor, and she's able to make her own decisions. And she wants to go home."

I looked outside at the glittering November day, the orange leaves still clinging to a few trees beyond the hospital, and I felt the unspeakable injustice of her being denied such precious time.

"Of course, I would prefer to see her stay for a few days. None of the tests are invasive, except the arteriogram, which uses some intravenous dye. The rest are scans and fairly simple. It would be helpful to know what we're dealing with."

"You mean helpful to you, but what about her?"

He didn't answer, but shrugged his shoulders.

"I know you're trying to do your job and help her, doctor, but I need to speak to her. It's got to be her decision, whether she has more tests—but personally, I'm against it."

I ended the conversation and went back to Mother's room. I found her eagerly waiting for me.

"Do you want more tests?" I asked without elaboration.

"No, Belva Ann. I want to go home."

"Good. Then I'll help you put your clothes on 'cause we're leaving."

***

Near the beginning of November Mother had her last chemo treatment. I sat with her while the nurse prepared the IV and a bag of toxins was infused into her body. She lay on a stiff bed, more like a table, the clear mixture dripping slowly into a vein. I wondered how, or why, she should take any more of this. She was becoming more and more exhausted, a tiredness that she said was virtually indescribable, unlike anything she could compare or relate to.

For now, we were merely cogs in a mechanical routine, visiting the office every three weeks, something we had been doing together since August, but I didn't see how it could continue much longer.

After her infusion the oncologist came in. He was Pakistani and somewhat difficult to understand. He felt her abdomen, asked a few questions, and then she sat up on the edge of the bed.

"I think," he said, "that we should stop the treatment."

He waited a moment, looking at Mother, then at me.

"I've looked at your test results and I really don't think we've made much of a difference. I'm sorry."

"So the tumors are growing?" asked Mother.

"Yes, I would say so…"

Mother looked over at me and I came to the table and took her hand. "Doctor, we've talked about this, and Mother has told me what she wants."

"I'd like to have Hospice," she said. "I don't want to go into a hospital again."

"Of course, Mrs. Penn. You're sure about this?"

"Yes. I just think I'd be better off at home, and my daughter here has said she could stay with me. I just want to be as comfortable as possible."

"Of course, of course. And I will write a recommendation to Hospice. They will be in touch with you."

"Thank you, Doctor," she said, touching his arm, "thank you for all you've done."

"I wish I could have done more, Mrs. Penn."

We left and walked to the car, the November sky growing overcast, clouds blowing in from the north.

"I'm hungry," she said. "Let's go to Wendy's."

I looked at her. "I can't believe it," I said, "that here you are, after all this, and you're thinking about lunch?"

"Why not?" she smiled. "Nothing's really changed. I just know now what I felt was happening anyway. And I still have to eat something…so do you."

So we did. We went to Wendy's, ordered burgers, and sat in the car, nibbling and talking. It was all so normal I thought—and this is how it is, no matter what the circumstances—you still have to eat, to sleep, to live. You have to do that till you're not living anymore. We were still living. She was still living.

I remembered to hold this thought as we sat in the car and watched the dark purple clouds gathering, tangling with the blue of the light-pierced sky.

Chapter Six

In the days that followed I began to notice the progression of Mother's disease in more profound ways. She was finding it harder to move about, to eat, to use the steps. In early evening when I'd help her to bed, she would lean heavily on me, taking the steps one or two at a time, then needing to sit down. It would take 15 minutes to get upstairs, longer to undress her as she lay exhausted on the bed.

I had gotten a plastic basin so she could get a sponge bath if she was too tired to use the bathroom. She would brush her teeth, I'd comb her hair, then she would roll over and quickly fall asleep, exhausted.

I realized that she wouldn't be able to do the stairs much longer, and a few days before Thanksgiving we prepared to move back to my parents' home, a small rancher on one floor.

It was an incongruously beautiful fall day as we left my house and drove across the lake. I knew it would be the last time, that she would not see the lake again. I knew too that she hated being dependent upon me, that she wanted me to go on with my life, yet this could not happen now. But I didn't care, for I would not have wanted to be anywhere else, wouldn't have chosen another place, another person, another moment but this. I wanted to be there for her, with her.

Mother and I returned home and Lew continued to live at the lake while Enjoué came with me. For awhile at least, it was easier this way. I took my father's old bedroom and moved a few of my clothes into his closet. It was an odd feeling to be in my parents' house, my father's house again, sleeping in his bedroom which had the smell of sandalwood and his Old Spice aftershave embedded in its comforter, its curtains, the fabric of the room. I felt ill at ease, like an interloper, until I realized how grateful Mother was to have me there.

"I couldn't get through this without you, Belva Ann," she said again and again. "I never realized how much I'd be needing you."

"I know—I'm glad I'm here," I would always respond. "Where else would I be?"

There seemed to be a small uplift in her spirits at being in her own home, and it was almost Thanksgiving—always a happy time for our family. Mother would ask friends and neighbors and distant relatives—we had no others—to join us, and she always baked a huge turkey and served it with all the seasonal trimmings. She loved doing it, and we loved eating it.

"I want to have Bob, and Mary and Verna here for Thanksgiving," she said one morning as I was tidying up her room.

"Mother—you're not up to that are you?"

"Yes, I am. I'd like to have another Thanksgiving in this house—and I want your father to come home for it. I probably won't be here for next year."

She had a tone in her voice that let me know she was adamant. I confess that between moving back home, scheduling the Hospice visitations, caring for Mother, closing up my studio, and trying to occasionally see my father, I was not particularly enthusiastic about cooking a big holiday meal. I envisioned a small turkey perhaps, a simple dinner for the three of us. And I was emotionally and physically becoming rundown myself.

But I looked at her and saw the determination in her eyes, all the memories of the happy holidays shared in this house welling up in them, and I couldn't say no. She was planning it already, before I even acceded to her wish.

"I want a big turkey—and you can get a good one at the market in Millville—and some stuffing—and I like to use the cornbread kind—and oh, I don't know—we could have a yam casserole and homemade relish—and your father likes pumpkin pies, not the mincemeat kind that Verna brings…"

I could see the meal morphing into an extravaganza at a time when nobody felt much like celebrating. I didn't even know if I could convince the hospital to let my father come home for the day, much less predict his behavior if he got there. I felt a certain apprehension in my body already.

"Okay," I said. "I will do it, but I don't know about Daddy. I'll do my best to see if he can come home, but I can't know what the doctors will say."

"Oh—please try," she pleaded.

***

It was the day before Thanksgiving and I was on the phone with the hospital for the third time. My calls were either not returned, or I was put on hold till the line went dead. I had become impatient and finally got through to the reluctant practitioner.

"Look," I said to the psychiatrist, growing weary of his evasions, "my father's wife, my mother, is dying. She may never have another holiday with us, and she's asking, begging, for him to come home. If he comes home and falls apart, then he'll be back at the hospital by 7PM regardless. It's only a few hours, but it would mean everything to her."

No response.

I was begging now too. Fill him up with Prozac, I thought, tell him he's being heroic, compassionate, whatever. But what I said was, "Just see if you can talk to him. See if he can spend a couple of hours with us. I'll take him back whenever he feels he wants to leave if it's too much for him. But please, just try."

"All right. I'll talk to him, but my primary concern has to be for his recovery, and I can't promise anything," he said.

I hung up the phone and while I waited on news of my father I directed my feeble culinary capabilities to the meal. Of course I had cooked holiday meals before, but never in a kitchen where every pan and spatula was either unfamiliar in my hands or tucked away in some obscure location that took long exasperating minutes to find.

Nothing was logical. The big turkey pan was in the basement in an overhead cupboard and wedged behind some stacks of rarely used pots and cookware. The family silverware was in a bedroom closet, behind a rack of women's shoes. Mother's fancy cut glass serving dishes were scattered among corner cupboards and hutches throughout the house. The turkey platter was in a big plastic bag in another storage space in the garage. Just assembling the cookware and serving dishes, even with Mother's instruction, proved daunting. Somehow, the night before Thanksgiving, I managed to set the table with china and crystal on my grandmother's antique embroidered tablecloth, and went to bed.

Thanksgiving morning Mother awakened me at 5 o'clock.

"Have you put in the turkey yet?" she asked.

I turned over, groggy and uncomprehending..."the turkey?"

"You need to get the turkey in the oven. It won't be done on time."

"Mother," I yawned, "it takes 3 hours." I glanced at the clock. "There's plenty of time."

"I've never made a turkey that didn't have to go for at least 6 or 7 hours," she said, contradicting me.

"I'll take care of it. Go back to bed." I groaned. "This is not a frozen bird. It takes three hours."

"What about the stuffing?" she persisted, still standing in the doorway.

Awake now I sat up and rubbed my eyes. "Mother, I make the stuffing in a separate casserole pan, so the turkey cooks faster. It'll be fine,"

But she wasn't giving up—"Well, it won't taste like much without the juice of the turkey. I don't know how to cook things that way."

I got up then and figured that my sleeping allotment was past. She was already in the kitchen, half-dressed with her housecoat falling off her nightgown, pulling out drawers, disgusted.

"What are you doing, Mother?"

"I'm going to start the yams."

"But we don't need to do that till later. Please sit down."

"No!" she shouted, more frustrated than I'd seen her during the whole illness. "*It's my kitchen. These are my things....and I want to do it.*" Tears streamed down her cheeks as she threw a pan down on the counter, then slumped over the sink. Her whole world was crumbling. She was losing control of everything. At that moment my concerns were of no importance. She could have this meal, I thought, in whatever way she wanted it. I would simply be an enabler.

"Okay, okay, I said as soothingly as I could. "We'll do whatever you want. You just tell me what you want me to do. You can help with whatever you would like."

Mother quieted down then and prepared the yams, baking them so they could later cool and be sliced into a casserole with brown sugar and cinnamon. I started shredding some cabbage for cole slaw while she told me how she wanted the dressing. The turkey went into the oven and I figured I could leave it on warm for a few hours if it threatened to be overcooked. After that, she was too tired to do anymore and went into the living room to lie down.

At noontime, Lew left for the hospital to pick up Father. Mother was eager, waiting in a wing chair by the door, looking at the street. When they arrived my father was smiling and more like himself. Mother and he kissed and gave each other a hug at the door. I felt tremendously relieved that he came back. What struck me, I guess, was the narrowness of his shoulders, the way his hair had whitened, the frailty of his appearance that found a resonance with what I had seen in Mina. It was a terrible thing he was going through for a man his age, to be in a hospital ward, separated from the life he knew. I hoped he would be able to come home soon, would *want* to come home.

He stood there inside the door, his hat in his hand, and looked like he wasn't sure where to go, as though this house, his house, was an unfamiliar place. Finally, seeing the rocker by the desk, he sat down heavily and the chair fetched back as it was prone to do. For a moment I thought he was going over, but he shakily righted himself then and sat without speaking.

Verna, Mother's cousin, tried valiantly to make conversation. She was in her seventies and wore heavy laced up shoes, a result of having polio as a young woman, and this had given her a dignity and a gentle perseverance. She was also a person more interested in others than herself, a trait that served her well that day as she plied my father with questions about his time on the coast, about the garden, the yard, the food at the hospital.

Lew had taken over cutting the grass and taking care of the exterior of the house, and I had assumed the paying of my parents' bills and dealing with the medical expenses. We were trying to maintain things for them as best we could. At least Father seemed to appreciate Lew's efforts on the yard and commented that "things look good outside."

Inside, overwhelmed and under-acknowledged, I struggled to pull the disparate elements of the meal together. By some good fortune, the turkey, the gravy, and all the side dishes made their appearance on cue. Bob and Mary appeared at 2PM and we all sat down to an elegant table, the china sparkling, my grandmother's silver, with a big arrangement of chrysanthemum cuttings and fall leaves centering the scene.

"Who wants to say grace?" asked Mother.

Nobody volunteered.

"I'll say grace," said Father, and began—

> *Oh Lord make us able,*
> *To eat all on the table;*
> *I know we can do it,*
> *If we only stick to it.*

It was his own personal prayer, repeatedly and humorously recited whenever there was a dirth of weightier religious sentiment. A few good-natured moans were heard, then Mother said, "Oh Belva Ann, you do it. You always say something nice."

I looked at my plate. A big lump immediately stuck in my throat. Here they all were, looking at me—a crippled woman, a mother dying of cancer, a father in a psychiatric ward, my husband and Bob and Mary sitting in stunned silence—and I couldn't find anything to say.

Finally I fell back on an old prayer—

> *Father, for the blessings*
> *we are about to receive,*
> *make us truly grateful.*

And barely able to articulate the words, my voice cracking, I added:

> *And for the gift of sharing this time together,*
> *we thank Thee.*

I could not look up at the faces around me. I knew that there would be an empty chair at the table next year, that there would not be another Thanksgiving.

"I'll get a pitcher of water," I said, going into the kitchen, turning on the water and wiping my eyes, seeing my mascara smearing on my fingertips. I swallowed back the lump in my throat and returned to the table where the turkey was being passed around and Verna was picking up the conversation. Bob and Mary and Mother were congratulating me on a beautiful dinner and forks were already clicking on china plates.

Everyone was busy enjoying the meal; Father was on his best behavior; and Mother played hostess, pushing serving dishes of food at everyone as soon as their plates began to empty. She was talking and eating, doing it almost frenetically, like she was playing a part, keeping a tradition, but it was somehow all a bit rushed and inappropriate...a façade...something that one does because it is expected. I knew that food wasn't tasting good to her now, and that she could enjoy very little.

I have no idea of the effort it must have taken her to hold together for that day, but at the end of the meal, when we all moved into the living room, she claimed the sofa and seemed to go limp. She was wearing a new red wool sweater I had bought for her, and gray tailored slacks. Her hair had been washed the day before by the health aide and she wore a bit of rouge and lipstick for the occasion, yet I noticed a cold sore forming on the corner of her mouth, and around her eyes there was a slight yellow tinge.

My father had eaten and was clearly eager to leave.

"I'm glad you came," she said, sitting up suddenly and looking at him as he prepared to return to the hospital with Lew.

He stared at her from the doorway and his face looked deeply sad. "You look bad, Mom," he said.

She paused and shook her head. "I know, John, I know. I can't help it."

I wished he had told her she looked nice. She had tried so hard to make this a good day. I wished he could say, "Your sweater's pretty," or "It's wonderful to see you again."

It was what it was. I could not change it.

I could see the sorrow on his face, but I could also see he wanted to leave. Mother went to the door and hugged him good-bye.

We heard the car start and slowly rumble out the driveway. It had been a very short visit.

"I'm sick," Mother said, suddenly turning to me as a mouthful of vomit fell on her new red sweater and she threw a hand over her lips. I ran for the kitchen and grabbed a pan and reached her just in time to see the undigested meal retched into the bowl. It was violent, an episode of projectile vomiting, and I held her forehead and tried to soothe her.

It happened very quickly but I was vaguely aware of the faces around me: Verna sitting rock still; Bob and Mary both looking away; no one talking; everyone trying to ignore what was happening. Why weren't they helping? Why wasn't anyone getting a towel with some cool water? Why weren't they gathering around to help? This was happening in their midst and they were immobile. I didn't understand it.

Finally, the retching stopped and I helped Mother to the bedroom where I washed her face and removed the soiled sweater. She fell on the bed and whispered that she needed to rest. It was dark then, and I went out and spoke to Bob and Mary and Verna.

"She needs to be quiet," I said.

"Such a shame," said Mary, shaking her head.

"Has this happened before?" asked Verna.

"No." I said. "This is the first time. She thinks she tried to eat too much all at once."

"It's getting late and we should leave anyway," Mary said. "Please call me if you need anything."

I knew she was sincere, but there was nothing really to do.

Thanksgiving was over. I turned to confront the dirty kitchen piled high with dishes and half-eaten plates of food. I couldn't begin to face it. I went to the garage, sat on the cellar steps in the coolness and the dark, and I sobbed.

Chapter Seven

The hospice people began appearing every few days now. Mother had a woman who was assigned to her case, and a visiting nurse who checked her once a week. The home health aide came on two afternoons each week to cook a meal and do some light housekeeping. Mother didn't want a stranger cleaning her house and preferred me to do it.

I always felt rushed and stressed, never having time to complete one chore before another would present itself, or a visitor would be at the door, or the phone would ring, or a nurse would appear, or Mother would need help with her clothes, her bath...

Christmas was only three weeks away and Mother had lists of people for whom she always bought gifts, and now she needed me to do the shopping for her. I tried to do this, knowing how much it meant to her to keep this tradition of giving. : It was however, the other list, the list she made for disposing of her possessions—the one describing who was to get her clothes, pieces of furniture, dishes and favorite items that troubled me.

"I want you and your father to have whatever you want," she said, "but after that, please give my friends a chance to pick out something for themselves."

I had never heard her speak of this before. "And I want you to know how I'd like to be dressed for my funeral."

"Oh, Mother...no," I interrupted, "we don't have to do this now..."

"No, honey," she stopped me firmly, putting a hand on

my arm, "yes, we do have to discuss this now. I want you to know these things; I *need* you to know what I want."

She reached into her closet and pulled out a navy blue silk dress, tailored and with tiny polka dots through the fabric, the kind of simple non-fussy garment that I had always associated with my mother. "And I'd like to wear some pearls, and a pair of comfortable shoes."

"I want Ed to sing at my funeral, that hymn he sang in church last year. I told him about it. He'll know the one. It was so beautiful. And I'd like a simple service, nothing too long. I don't want people to have to sit through some lengthy sermon." She paused and looked at me very earnestly. "Promise me you'll remember."

"I will," I said, trying not to cry yet again.

"And please keep an eye on your father. I don't know what will become of him."

"Yes, I'll do that...but after how he's behaved...well, I guess I've never felt about him the way I feel about you. You were always there for me." I was still angry with him for leaving her this way in her illness.

"I don't know," she said, "I just don't know what he's thinking. I don't know what he'll do."

And we let the subject end there.

I went into the kitchen to blow my nose and make us some tea. I reached for the Dilaudid, the pain killer that had been prescribed for Mother, along with the anti-nausea medication. She was having "a little distress" now, as she described it, and hospice had been good about getting her the new medications which I gave her regularly.

As I made a tray to take to the bedroom I looked about me. The house was decorated for Christmas, bows and wreaths and garlands draping a house of immeasurable sorrow. I wondered at the incongruity of it, wondered why I had bothered to do it, the color and greenery masking the tragedy that surrounded us. I couldn't hold it comfortably in my mind. Everything seemed wrong. I made the tea quickly and returned to her room.

"Oh, look at the snow!" she said.

I looked out the window to see big snowflakes like filigreed cut-paper gliding past the panes. The flakes were so dense that they obscured the view of the neighboring houses and the street beyond.

"Oh," she said, entranced, "I never thought I'd see the snow again!"

We stood at the window together and I could see she was smiling, joyful, and I thought the Dilaudid had altered her mood, that maybe it was that first morphine rush where everything feels inexplicably wonderful. Whatever it was, she began reciting:

> *The snow had begun in the gloaming,*
> *And busily all the night,*
> *Was heaping field and highway,*
> *In a silence deep and white.*

These were the lines of her favorite poem by James Russell Lowell, "The First Snowfall"... I had heard it all my life and treasured it.

"I think I'd like some breakfast now," she said, very bright and cheery. "I feel a little better today I think."

"Well—what would you like?" I asked, happy for her.

"Maybe a soft-boiled egg over a piece of white toast."

"Your wish is my command," I joked, saluting, then marching out the door.

In the kitchen I put two eggs in a pot to boil, one for her and one for me. As the steam started to rise off the pan I thought of my father and his love of boiled eggs—and how I used to hate them.

We had chickens when I was a kid, and I always gathered the eggs from the little wall boxes filled with straw out in the poultry house where they all roosted. I could still recall the strong ammonia and straw smells that emanated from the roosts. And I never particularly liked the eggs.

Sometime when I was in second or third grade my father impulsively wrote a poem in pencil on my egg before he boiled it. It was a four-line verse, long forgotten now, but I could not read it unless I agreed to eat the egg. This I did, and after that, every weekend when I'd come down for breakfast, there would be another poem waiting, usually about something funny that happened during the week—some event, some person—and always in good meter, perfectly rhymed.

We soon began to call these missives "The Egg Poems" and my mother would write them on a file card before I cracked the eggs apart. Always they were clever, always they made us laugh, and my father took a certain humorous pride in them, sometimes sharing the poems with friends.

I'll never know how he did it. Some of the verses were so intricate—12 and 16 line stanzas—all written in his beautiful handwriting reduced to the miniaturized surface of an egg.

When my parents moved to a smaller house in retirement, the poems were somehow lost. I wished I had them. I also wished my father were home with us.

Lew, at least, was encouraging, saying he was doing better. He was making some gadgets in the woodshop therapy class. My father was always handy that way, and mechanical, and this gave him something to do with his time. I knew in his youth that he was also musical, had played trumpet with a Dixieland band and sung in a quartet. I'm not sure where all this talent came from, because I doubt that he had much encouragement at home as a boy. I'm certain he never had music lessons, and he never was even allowed to finish high school. In his teens he had to work at a lumber yard to help support his family. But by his mid-twenties, working hard, he had pulled enough savings together to start his own service station. In his early thirties he married my mother.

I looked at the steaming eggs and removed them from the

pan, putting Mother's on a piece of buttered toast, and returned to her room. She was lying down again, dressed, and staring at the ceiling.

"Do you see them?" she asked as I put down the tray.

"See who?"

"Up there." She pointed toward the ceiling.

"What's up there?" I asked, trying to fathom what she was referring to.

"The cats," she said. "You don't see them?"

I looked up again, feeling a prickling sense on my spine. "No, I don't see anything."

"They're cats. Cat faces," she said, still staring.

"Are they scary?" I asked.

"No...they're kind of cute. They're smiling, sort of."

"Oh," I said, "Well, I'm glad. Maybe they're just keeping you company."

"You really don't see them?" she asked again, skeptically.

"No, but I'm sure they're just fine." I said, trying to humor her. "Let's sit you up so you can have your breakfast."

I put some pillows behind her back. "Oh look," she said, "the snow has stopped."

So it had, but a thin coating of white lay on the ground, the first snowfall, softening the contours of the trees, the ground, and the slippery bird feeder where Pete the Squirrel was working outside to steal some of the last seeds. It would not snow again till long after Christmas.

Chapter Eight

"It's all normal," the hospice nurse said. "We expect these things."

*All normal...*I mull it over. *Nothing is normal,* I think, yet my mind takes up the phrase because it seems to diminish my sense of being fearful, of being inadequate to help her, to save her.

Mother has jaundice, a result of her liver shutting down, but it is normal. In her mouth resides a carpet of sores, but it is a thrush infection, and normal as her immune system collapses. Her feet and ankles are swelling, her body retaining fluid, but it too is normal at this stage of disease.

I study the hospice people who deal with death and dying and know that for them, this is routine. Yet there is nothing predictable, certain, right, fair, or normal about what is happening to my mother. It is not normal to me.

"Yes. We can give you a liquid for her to swish and swallow, something to help with the thrush," they say. "And it helps the edema to elevate her feet a few hours a day." And "We will be here for you," they say. Then they are gone.

It is not fair, I tell Lew, not fair that she has become so weak, so emaciated, and now she must suffer all these physical indignities. She has been through enough.

Mother does not complain. She is cooperative with me and with the hospice nurse. She is still trying to eat, usually a small cup of broth, or a piece of toast with warm milk and butter on it. Nothing else agrees with her.

She is finding it harder to bathe and has had nothing but

sponge baths for two weeks. She wants a tub bath again and I try to help her. As I watch her undress I realize that I have not seen my mother completely naked since Thanksgiving. She takes off her nightgown and I am shocked. There is no comparative to what I am seeing except images of people in concentration camps or starving refugees. Her skin is stretched over bone; all the muscle is gone. The vertebrae of her spine stand out in a sharp ridge between knife-like shoulder blades. Her legs are the thickness of my arms.

I sponge soap and water across her back and avert my eyes. It is too painful to see her this way. She is only in the tub a couple of minutes and already growing tired. I hurry and go into the hall closet for a towel. From the corner of my eye I see she is trying to rise, grabbing the sides of the tub, but she cannot pull herself up.

"I can't do it," she says. "I can't get out."

I try to lift her, but even thin as she is, she is dead weight. "See if you can get onto your knees," I tell her, "and I will get in the tub with you and help you stand."

She does this, turning over and struggling as the towel and the wet sponge flop on the floor. I'm afraid she will fall. I get in the tub with my shoes still on and tell her to put her arms around my neck. Then I grab her around the waist and pull her up.

She cries out, "Oh"—and I feel I've hurt her.

We stand there, both wet and gasping. "Are you okay?" I ask, frightened.

"Yes," she says, "but I can never do this again."

I know she is right.

I help her back to her bedroom, the water in my shoes sloshing down the hall. As we turn into her room, I feel we have crossed a border, and there will be no going back.

***

Two weeks before Christmas my father came home. The

psychiatrist told him the time ahead was going to be very hard, and he would need to continue to see him as an outpatient once a week.

As I drove my father from the hospital he seemed subdued. He showed me the keyholder he had made in woodshop. It was a little piece of sanded plywood in the shape of a key, varnished, and with several hooks screwed where keys should hang. I couldn't tell if he was proud of it. They weren't allowed to use the jigsaw to cut it, he said, but he had done the rest. It was unspeakably sad—my father—a man who had built cabinetry, put in our heating system, done complicated mechanical work all his life—was screwing hooks into plywood. I told him the keyholder was nice and he could decide where to hang it in the house when we got back. Then he asked about Mother and said again that he thought "this would all be over when I got home." I felt that he wanted "it" to be all over, and despite everything, I resented the remark.

"She needs you, Daddy, needs *us*, and it's good that you are here," I said, pushing down the anger.

Mother was in her bedroom sleeping when my father came home, reclaiming his old room, walking around the yard, checking the basement, and settling into some semblance of his old life. He did not overtly show any emotion at the situation in which he found himself. He was taking medication which decreased his anxiety, but it also made him sleepy, and he sat in his recliner, a book in his hand, and napped a lot during those first days. He was not permitted to drive yet, thankfully so, and I was grateful that Bob and Mary lived within walking distance and that he had their company and that of neighbors who were fond of stopping by.

He was content to leave Mother's care to me. Mother was in bed most of the time now. She needed help to get to the bathroom and to occasionally walk into the living room in the evenings. The decline in the past two weeks had been profound. Still, one is never really prepared.

As she lay on the bed that morning, her eyes closed, I

slipped in and tidied up her bathroom, scouring the sink and putting out some clean towels and hand cloths. I was quiet, trying not to disturb her, when she suddenly said very clearly, "I think I'll say good-bye to you now, Belva Ann."

I ran to the bed, "Oh, oh no...not now..."

She was staring, seeing and feeling something I could not discern. I fell into the bed beside her, holding her as close as I could. I felt that I was holding onto something, someone, very small, a shadow almost, and that she was impossibly slipping away. At that moment I could not grasp her close enough, could not help her, stop her, keep her. I heard the beating of a heart and did not know to whom it belonged, yet miraculously, we still both breathed.

I rose up on my elbow then and looked into her face, impassive, serene, and with a wordless question clouding her eyes. She spoke then.

"I guess.....I guess I just felt for a minute that I was...going," she said.

"Oh, Mommy, are you in pain?" I asked, trembling.

"No, no pain...I'm just feeling awfully...hollow inside."

We lay there, me holding her, and both of us in tears. After awhile she seemed to drift off into some kind of half-sleep. I carefully tiptoed out and sat alone on the sunporch. I was shaken and stunned.

Oh God, I asked, *how can this be happening?* I wasn't ready to say good-bye. I wasn't ready for any of it.

Enjoué came over then and put her head on my knee. I rubbed her ears and stroked her wet nose.

She needs a walk, I thought to myself. I had neglected her all morning. Little needs, little routines, but they forced me from the sorrow. I told the health aide I was leaving for awhile.

"Come on, girl," I said, "let's go out for a walk." I wanted then to be under the trees, inexplicably just wanted to be out, under the pine trees in the woods at the end of the street, the ones that smelled so fragrant in the chill air. Their branches always calmed the wind as it passed. I remembered the pine trees in the woods where I grew up—their soft blankets of needles, the sweep of lower branches where I could climb, and hide, their evergreen smells enveloping me. There was always a peacefulness there, and the memory of it comforted me. I would return to the house a little later, and I would try to carry the presence of the pine trees with me.

Chapter Nine

Ghosts. There were ghosts in the house that December. They were in the hallway, sometimes at the foot of her bed. She saw Uncle Sherm and Aunt Abbie coming to visit her. She heard him say, "Hello, little girl," in his affectionate way. She smiled at that. Cousin Leroy was sometimes with them, all of them long dead.

"Does this happen?" I asked the hospice nurse and the volunteer.

"Yes," the nurse responded. "It happens a lot. People who are dying often see their loved ones."

"She's hallucinating then?"

"Who's to say?" she said kindly. "They may be there."

I decided to believe they were there, that they were surrounding us, waiting.

"Are you going to be able to do this?" the nurse asked of me then. I was exhausted and probably looking terrible.

"Yes," I said, "I can do this." I prayed at least that I could. I was sleeping on a wooden settee in the TV room since Daddy had moved back. It was too short for me to stretch out, an uncomfortable antique, and I was sleeping poorly.

Then there was the bell. Mother had fallen a few days before trying to get to the bath unassisted. She was unhurt, but after that I had given her a dog bell to ring when she needed to get up. The bell rang much of the day, and three or four times a night, and all of it, I suppose, was wearing me down. It was insignificant however to what she was going through, and every day brought another change, another diminishment, another loss of something she valued.

"How do you think it will happen?" I asked the nurse, worried. "The doctors said she would probably go into a coma and simply slip away." It was the best outcome I could think of now.

"We can hope for that," she said, "but we really don't know."

I promised to call her immediately if there was any change. I hugged her and Mother's faithful volunteer, thanked them both. I knew I would see them in a few days, sooner if needed.

Mina was calling everyday now, as were Mother's best friends, and Mary and Bob stopped in every night. While Bob sat with Father, Mary would go into the bedroom and sit with Mother for awhile. She would come out, stand in the hall, and silently cry.

It was becoming evident that we needed a hospital bed, and so hospice ordered one and put it in the bedroom. We could raise and lower it to help Mother sit up so her lungs wouldn't fill with fluid. I sat on the side of Mother's bed and held her hand when it was noisily assembled, metal bars and braces and clanking cranks grinding into place. She watched it as one watches a cage entering a room, a place of confinement. I hated it. I felt she did. It was a symbol of something despised, but we needed it now.

***

It was the middle of December, and she was screaming at me. I had never seen her this way during her whole illness. All the despair was being funneled into rage.

"Take me to the hospital," she yelled reproachfully at me. "I can't go to the bathroom, can't eat...This is no life. Put me in a hospital!"

"Mother," I begged, "you don't want that. Remember what we talked about? You can be more comfortable at home."

"I want to go to the hospital!" she screamed, desperate. "I want them to knock me out!"

I went into the kitchen and called the hospice nurse. "Mother is frantic," I said. "Please come right away."

I ran back into the room but she was out of bed, naked, laying on the floor between the bedroom and bath. "Mother!" I gasped, stooping to help her.

"No—let me go. Let me go. I want to be left here!"

I tried to lift her up and she struck out at me with her fist. I was shocked and backed away. "I can't leave you on the floor like this. Please...." I was more tired than I've ever been in my life. "And you're hitting me, being horrible to me!" It sounded weak, silly, mean, and I felt enormously guilty.

"I'm dying." She screamed back enraged.

"I know. But that doesn't give you the right to be so mean!" After I said it I was instantly appalled, depressed, upset with myself. I tried to help her again and she angrily pushed my arm away. I hardly recognized her, or me.

From somewhere Uncle Bob appeared then, and he stood in the doorway, shocked at the scene before him.

"Please help me," I begged.

We both got Mother back into bed. I was so disgusted with myself, yet a part of me was glad he saw her this way. I wanted someone to see, someone to know the monumental horror we were living. I was selfish, and I hated myself for it. It was also survivor's guilt; I was living and my mother was dying.

I covered her in a blanket and she threw it off, kicked it away. The covers were her enemies. The whole room was her place of rage. Soon the nurse came, and she motioned me out and closed the door.

I sat on the sunporch, trembling. I didn't know what to do anymore. I was becoming something, someone, I didn't know. There was no uninterrupted time, and when there were a few hours, I was too exhausted to care. My old life, the one of teacher and artist seemed as remote from me as a dream. I had willingly given it up, given up my home, given up time with my husband, and now I didn't know what I had become. I wanted to be here for her, for both of them, yet I felt like I was collapsing into a whirlpool and I couldn't swim.

After about a half hour the nurse came out and motioned me into Mother's room. She was quiet, under the covers, looking resigned.

"I told your mother that we can give her medication and keep her comfortable here, much more than they would do in a hospital. She has said she wants to stay."

I looked at my mother as I stood at the foot of the bed. "I'm sorry," she said, appearing so small that I could barely believe there was a human being under the covers; there was hardly any rise in the blanket where she lay.

"I'm sorry too," I said, clutching the foot of the bed. I speechlessly walked the nurse to the door.

"I don't think it can be much longer," she said, pausing as she stood in the chilly open doorway. "This is the last battle. It's usually the anxiety as death approaches, the last struggle. I think she'll be calmer now." Then seeing my tears, laying a hand on my arm she said, "You're doing a good job. Stay strong."

"Thank you for coming," I replied in a shaky voice.

***

December 19th was the last day Mother wrote in her notebook, a little pad where she kept lists of things she needed, thank you cards she wanted to send, snippets of favorite sayings or poetry. It was also the last day she had anything to eat, although she could still take her medicines with a few sips of water.

In the living room, the room of the living, a tree was decorated in red felt birds as it had always been at Christmas. One white dove sat on the topmost branch, and underneath there were presents wrapped and donned with bows, scattered among the tiny reindeer and felt toys my father had as a boy.

"It's so beautiful," she said as I helped her into the room to see the tree. "You've done so much," she said, smiling at me, "and I wanted to see it all again." She went back to the room then and I knew she was slipping away, leaving us, drawing into herself.

After that she spoke little, and when she did it was barely audible. She rang the bell less and less, no longer able to get out of bed even when assisted. I used diapers and disposable bed coverings that I changed several times a day. When she couldn't lift herself using the bed's handrails, I changed the bedding by rolling her onto her side as the nurses had shown me, making the bed one portion at a time.

"I never thought you'd be doing this for me," she whispered once.

"Why not?" I said, kissing her ear. "You did it for me."

She didn't answer, and it was like completing a circle, I thought. We enter the world and we can't speak, can't eat food, can't control our bodily functions—and we go back to the same place in life at which we once came in. "I came as a child"...the words of a sermon heard one forgotten Christmas whispered in my head... "and I left as a child,"... I completed the thought as I looked at her.

Our little family drew together then, tightening the circle as the rest of the world trended away. The phone stopped ringing, the neighbors and friends stopped visiting. My own friends too stopped calling. They respected in some unspoken way that this was a time for those closest; a sacred passage.

Three days before Christmas, Mother lapsed into a coma. That night I went silently into her room, pulling a chair up close to her bed, and reading her my Christmas card. At the end, I said, "It's Christmas, Mother," and I kissed her forehead and saw her lips move slightly, and I felt that somewhere in the depths into which she was descending, she understood. I wanted her to know that it was okay to go, to leave us then.

As I left the room my father came in to sit with her.

I only wanted to be somewhere quiet and alone, and I went out of the house where I sat on the steps leading into the garage. It was cold there, the steps damp and hard, the concrete unforgiving. Glancing about I saw my old sled hanging on a hook overhead, the one I had used in so many childhood winters. I remembered the crunch and gravelly sifting of the snow as it slid under the blades, the way the runners bounced over frozen ground and the rough chunks of ice that fell from the trees. And I remembered the Christmas that my parents took me for a sled ride up the little unpaved road through the woods, the one that went all the way from our house to the outskirts of Millville.

It was dark and quiet as my parents pulled me along, my leggings and boots lightly flecked with snow, with the stars blinking through the arms of the trees. It seemed to me that the world around was sleeping, holding its breath. The only sounds were my parents' footsteps and the shush of my sled in the snow, or an occasional crackling of an icy branch somewhere in the forest. We passed unseen in the starlight, the thin haze of our breath misting the air.

It was a wondrous night. There was a beauty about it, a mystery in the snow and the night sky. And it was Christmas. When we reached the old railroad tracks on the edge of town my father suggested we turn back. It was cold and late, but we returned singing "Jingle Bells" and "Silent Night," and as we sang we could hear faint echoes of our voices in the woods. Sometimes we would stop, startled, listening.

It was a perfect night, a perfect moment. I thought of it then, held all of its presence in the sight of a wooden sled, battered and rusting in the garage, its logo fading like the snows of that long distant Christmas. But it was still there, in my mind, that singular precious moment, and I smiled through tears, remembering.

***

It was 5 o'clock in the morning when Lew came to my door and said, "Belva Ann, I think you should come now." I was instantly awake, knowing what he meant. We had kept a vigil for two days, Lew, my father, and me. We didn't want her to ever be alone. I walked quickly down the hall and saw my father hovering over the edge of the bed.

"Her breathing's changed," he said as I entered.

I waited for what seemed a long time till she took a shallow breath, then I pulled a wooden chair up to the bed and took her hand.

"It's okay, Mommy," I said, we're all here." I looked across at my father who seemed restrained, but his eyes were full and red, like he was trying to hold all the emotion inside. He reached out and took her other hand.

We watched as her breaths grew very far apart, and we would wait, hardly breathing ourselves until she took another. Her mouth was closed, eyes closed; she seemed incredibly peaceful. If there was a battle raging for life, it was passed now, beyond our vision. Everything was slowing down with the breaths—a softness, a tentativeness surrounding us.

It is an unequivocal thing to see a life ending, the finality of it, of being, the death of a store of experiences, hopes, sorrows, loves, memories, all drifting into some unknown absent place. There can be nothing more significant, nothing that forces such a knowledge of our frailty, our impermanence, our short participation in the ravenous and beautiful dance of life. This is the vigil, I thought, of those who wait, of those who love by the final gift of their presence.

It was dark outside and I went to a bedroom window and opened the curtains. I wanted the light to come in. I wanted her to be able to follow the light.

I went back to the bed and bowed my head on the blanket—I was not religious, none of us were—but I began to say the 23rd Psalm, the one I learned years ago in Sunday school. I saw again the kindly image of the Shepherd, leading his flock through the Valley of Death. If she could hear, I wanted her to know this.

I heard my father's voice joining with my own. We finished and looked up at each other. The breathing had become very shallow, each breath more distant than the last. There was no struggle, no gasping, no marker to note that a boundary had been crossed. There was simply a fading, as gently palpable as a breeze that lightly passes, leaving only a sense of displacement, then a silence.

The passage to death, I realized, was hard to define, discreetly unremarkable. Her face was the same, her hands the same, everything looked as it had, and yet she had left us, and we stood by the bed and watched her go. I still held onto her hand and stayed with her. My father kissed her good-bye and went into his bedroom, closing the door. I heard him softly sobbing. Lew went out into the hall and left me alone.

It was 6:20 in the morning. Grey light faintly filtered through the bedroom windows. It barely illuminated the trees and the street outside, the houses where a few Christmas candles still glowed in the dim morning. It was Christmas Eve; it was my wedding anniversary; and it was now, and for as long as I lived, something more. It was the day my mother died.

Chapter Ten

The morning of the funeral was overcast and cold. The service was in Leesburg, the same place where we had buried my Uncle Sherm and my grandfather thirty-three Decembers ago. It all seemed at once vaguely familiar and desolately foreign.

Yet everything was as she wanted it: a short eulogy, the blue polka dot dress, the bouquet of daisies, the pearls, and Ed singing. My parents' friends, my friends, were there. The hospice volunteers came. "Grief shared is grief diminished," they said, but I didn't feel that then. I was swallowed in loss. I could hardly bear to see my mother's coffin committed to the frozen ground.

A few snowflakes drifted over the windshield as we rode back home. There was a reception to prepare at the house. People needed to gather and talk. I had to be a hostess. My father went into his bedroom and fell face down, sprawled on the bed, crying. I rubbed him on the back and asked him if he could come out and talk to people. He didn't respond so I closed the door and left him alone. I couldn't give in to more tears, not with people waiting in the living room. Somehow we got through the afternoon. It was a long day.

After the funeral I stayed on with my father for a few days, but finally, when I could stay no longer, I asked him if he'd like to come back with me to the lake.

"No," he said, "I'd rather be here, where your mother is." I thought his tense of the verb was strange, but then, this had been their home of many years. It was familiar, I thought, and he needed time to adjust.

I was glad to be going back to my home. I was exhausted, emotionally and physically. I slept for two days, getting up only to have a cup of tea or soup, and returning to the darkness of my room to sleep again. Then, on the third day, I saw a commode full of blood.

I couldn't believe it; I stared in horror. I tried to be calm but I was terrified. Maybe it won't happen again, I thought, desperately, hopefully.

But it did happen, and a couple of days later I was seeing Dr. Rieser and his face was grave.

"I think you should have some tests," he said, studying me seriously, "definitely a sigmoid or a barium test, and I want to order some X-rays and blood tests as well."

The only word that I really heard clearly was "barium." I remembered my mother, her distress at that procedure, and the specter of colon cancer that seemed to hang over his words. She was buried less than a week, and this was happening now, to me.

I felt frightened, in an almost irrational, primitive way, yet I felt that this was something I deserved, as though I needed to go through some form of penance because I had lived while my mother had died. I deserved the pain. It made no sense, but I realized that nothing made any sense to me anymore. And as it was, I had no options. I was too alarmed and too tired to question Dr. Rieser.

***

When colour goes home into the eyes,
And lights that shine are shut again...

I held the book in my shaking hands—the hands that had the same patterns of veins, the same wrinkled creases and narrow tapered fingers as my mother's—and I read the opening lines of "The Treasure" by Rupert Brooke, the poem that was read at her funeral. It was one that I loved and the words spoke to me of her, of the store of memories she had bequeathed to me.

A nurse came by and said they were ready to take some blood. I put the book away and went down to phlebotomy. The technician looked at my arms, my hands, puzzling over where to find a vein. She tightened a tourniquet about my arm and poked and prodded, then made an inept stab, struggling, wriggling the needle backward and forward.

I winced. "If you can't do this, please get someone who can. I won't be poked again."

She left and another technician appeared. "So you have veins that are difficult?" he said.

"Yes, I have difficult veins." It sounded ridiculous, but it was true, and I repeated the phrase with a fatalistic certitude.

He studied my arm and eased a needle in, hitting the mark effortlessly, and I saw my blood flowing into a series of color-coded vials.

"That takes care of it," he said.

I thanked him and left for the X-ray department, blood oozing through the cotton patch on my arm. I felt as I did when I was three and left in the merciless ward of a hospital, sick with whooping cough, measles, and mumps—all at once. The doctors thought it was leukemia, and the relentless nurses came to extract my blood every day. I was abandoned and helpless, and I didn't understand why. Now as I was strapped to a table, I felt the same vulnerable emotions again.

"This is a balloon," the nurse said. "It will hold the barium line in place for the enema." It felt as though a golf ball was being inflated inside my rectum. I was just a hunk of flesh now, I thought, but one that felt pain, and breathed, and was trembling. Then I was pumped up with an unknown liquid and intermittent puffs of air and told to hold it all as I was rotated before an X-ray machine, still strapped down.

The nurses and technicians left the room then, removed themselves as I was bombarded with unseen blasts of radiation. So this is what she went through, I thought. She endured this. How horrible it must have been for her, this test, and with the obstruction of a cancer growing in her colon.

Sometime later the lab assistant came in—"Oh, no need to cry," she said. "It's all over now."

Poor woman, she didn't know, couldn't know, why I was so upset.

I quickly dressed and drove home, immediately going to the bath where I lay in the tub for an hour, letting the benison of hot water wash over me. I wanted to remove every trace of the barium, the touch of the metal gurney, the memory of the hospital from my body. Afterwards I fell into bed and did not get up again until Lew came home. It was dark then, and I threw my arms around him and cried inconsolably.

For a week I remained in bed, feeling terrible, carrying a morbid premonition that I was destined to travel the same horrific path as my mother. My hopelessness was all-consuming, along with the bottomless fatigue.

I slept in the guestroom where Mother had stayed. I hadn't been able to change the sheets, and the bed still smelled of her presence there, her skin, her soap. I found it a small comfort, and I rested in a kind of suspended space as I waited for news from the doctor. Finally it came.

***

"So, how did the tests go?" my father asks. He is sitting in a wing chair when I come in, not reading, not watching TV, just staring out the front picture window.

"They went fine," I say smiling. "The doctor called and said I have colitis. I need to get some rest and watch my diet for certain things." I don't add that I need to avoid anxiety.

(That seems too much to hope for.)

"Well, that's good then." He seems genuinely pleased and relieved.

"Yes, that's *very* good.....," I reply, observing speechlessly that he looks like a statue, like he's been sitting there immobile for a long time. "But now, how are *you*?" I ask.

"Oh, I'm doin' all right."

"Are you sure?" I press, leaning in toward him.

"Well, the house is awfully lonely without your mother." He has tears swelling in his eyes. "You know, sometimes at night, I think I hear her calling to me."

I feel I should go over and hug him, but I don't. He showed so little sorrow when she was sick...and now this. I notice he is breathing heavily again, and there's a strange metallic, sour smell in the house. I presume it is his breath, probably from the Haldol, the medication prescribed for him.

"It's hard," I say. I am at a loss for any more words or I too will cry.

"What have you been doing with your time?" I ask, changing the subject.

"Oh, I don't know, I'm just trying to keep the house picked up and putting things away."

I can see the room is looking spare, my mother's beloved little arrangements of plates and porcelain sculptures, her antique stoneware crocks of dried flowers—all removed. The Christmas decorations are down; even the wreaths on the doors are gone. It looks like the house is being stripped to utilitarian barrenness. I say nothing. Instead, I compliment him on how neat and tidy everything is.

"Well, I can't do things like your mother would do," he says, somewhat apologetically.

"You don't have to, Daddy," I offer, trying to be encouraging. "You have to do things the way you want them."

He looks awkward and switches the conversation to another topic. "The hospice nurse...you know, *that* woman...she was here and she wants me to go to the Senior

Center with her. I told her I won't go." He looks defensive.

"I understand," I say, "It's awfully soon, but maybe later, after a little time, you'll feel like it. They have a lot of people there like yourself, a lot of nice activities they offer."

He is ignoring me, looking out the window again. I'm sure the subject is closed for awhile.

I worry about him, worry about what he's doing with himself, worry that he's spending too much time alone. I, too, am feeling enclosed in my own grief. I tell myself that it's part of the withdrawal, the seclusion we all need to go through after such a great loss. It will take a long time, and nothing will ever be the same for any of us.

I know my father is still not interested in driving, and this is certainly contributing to his isolation. Lew, or myself, or Bob and Mary need to get his groceries and pick up his prescriptions every week. I go through his mail and continue to pay the household and medical bills, filling out the information, then having him laboriously sign the checks. He does not like this arrangement. He thinks I should go to the local office of each company and personally present myself to pay his bills, something he used to do years ago before Mother took over. I cannot impress upon him that things are seldom done that way anymore.

At least once a week, Lew and I bring him up to our home for dinner, then take him to his appointment with the psychiatrist. They usually talk for an hour. The doctor thinks he is making good progress. I am glad he has this continued contact.

Through all of this, however, I can't discern if he is grateful for our efforts or not, though he seems generally content with the situation and has expressed no inclination toward greater independence. Occasionally he seems to think the police have an interest in him, and I wonder why he continues to fixate on the police rather than on the time he nearly killed Mother in an Ocean City parking lot? Or pinned me against a garage wall?

Perhaps it is an aspect of selective memory, of forgetting or minimizing the most unpleasant of our shortcomings and experiences. I realize I'm still feeling angry with him, still resentful that he had been so completely willing to abandon Mother at a time when she was still able to enjoy a few things in life. And when her physical condition began to decline, he had been more than eager to leave her care to me, to be out of the house, to be done with everything. I suppose you could call it his weakness, his personal flaw, a mental disease—or all of these—but I was still grappling with the fact that he had simply left her adrift. Since her death I had been trying to be a dutiful daughter, but it would take awhile to heal my own internal rifts and questionings about why these things had happened.

Then there was the other aspect, the less flattering one about me, something which I was beginning to suspect had held me together emotionally. I had, perhaps, been angry at my father because it left less room for feeling the pain of the impending loss of my mother. Anger, I discovered, left little room for other emotions. It was a temporary fix, a release, an escape from a greater sorrow. Somehow, I needed to get past this; I knew I needed to somehow let this all go and try to begin again.

***

"Your mother is at peace now, and God has added a thousand stars to your crown," my friend Liz Sherman wrote. She had been a good support to me, an artist and painting companion, a former neighbor, and an immeasurable source of comfort during difficult days. I was grateful for all of my friends, but when I read her beautiful letter, and another from fellow artist George Cheety, I felt surrounded by love. George's father had died in January, and he too was in his own grief, yet he had generously reached out to me. Liz's mother was ill with Alzheimers, yet her concern for others was extraordinary. I found comfort in their words, in their efforts to say more than the usual banalities about death and loss.

I had few spiritual beliefs, but I clung to the kindnesses of those who did, and I tried to find a way to live with the presence of all-enveloping sadness. I busied myself writing thank-you notes to those who had helped us, managed errands and responsibilities for Father, and tried to rebuild some semblance of my former life. I picked up some paintings where I had left off in November, took Enjoué on walks in the snow, began to see a few of my friends again, and I tried to help my father with his legal affairs and with probating Mother's will.

***

On an afternoon in mid-January my father and I sat in the office of our family's attorney, a man who had known my parents and grandparents for 50 years. He was a soft-spoken, intelligent person, friendly, immaculately groomed and a bit smooth as only lawyers can be.

"It's a fairly simple will," he said soothingly. "Everything in your wife's estate goes to you, John, and upon your death to Belva Ann."

"What about the house?" asked my father. "Do I get to stay there?"

The attorney looked quizzical and cast a glance at me. "Of course," he said. "It's your home that you and Belva owned jointly. Don't you want to stay there?"

"Well, yes, I guess so," said my father, then added, "as long as they'll let me." He looked at me with that distrustful gaze I'd seen before, as though he needed my permission. I swallowed hard and told him I wanted him to stay there for as long as he was able, then looked back at the attorney.

"I see you don't have a Power of Attorney, do you, John?

Or someone who could pay your bills, handle legal affairs, speak for your wishes if you could no longer do so?"

"No, I guess not."

"And you should have a Health Care Surrogate too. I see that Belva named Belva Ann to that role back in September."

I closed my eyes and thought about the day Mother and I went to a notary in Sea Isle, the one who authorized the papers. It was only four months ago—yet a lifetime it seemed. Mother was so worried she might need assistance then and she trusted me without question.

"Well...does that mean she could put me away?" my father asked, pulling me back to the present.

I gasped. The attorney looked shocked, but he knew my father was paranoid, knew the history, and tried to mollify the situation.

"I think this is in everyone's best interest," he said, noting that he had even signed such papers giving Power of Attorney to his own daughters. He said it made it easier for a family member to deal with property or medical decisions.

My father seemed to trust him, but definitely not me. "You're sure—you say this is the best thing—?" he asked uncertainly.

"Yes. You've known me a long time, John, and I think this is best."

"Okay then," my father conceded, signing the documents before him.

I felt a sense of enormous relief that this much was done, but I also felt distressed that after everything that had happened, he would somehow still not trust me, his only daughter.

I drove my father home and didn't say a word. I knew he still had mental issues, but some part of me was beyond feeling disgusted. Some part of his behavior seemed disturbingly, maddeningly, willful. I wondered why all his paranoia centered on me.

When we got back to the house, Bob and Mary stopped

by. We talked for a brief while, but I needed to leave as it was nearly dinnertime and I had had a long day.

"I feel like a hamburger from McDonald's," said my father, addressing me as I headed toward the door, viewing me, I supposed, as his errand girl.

"Don't you have anything to eat here in the house?" I asked.

"I don't bother cookin' much. I just eat me some canned mushroom soup every night."

"What do you mean...you don't try to heat anything else? That's not very healthy." I said, staring at him.

"Well...I don't feel like much."

"But you feel like a hamburger now, if I'll take another hour and go get it for you?"

No reply.

"Sorry, Daddy," I said. "But I'm tired too. You need to learn to heat a TV dinner or a frozen meal once in awhile...and I need to get home."

I turned on my heels as I heard Mary say, "I'll go get you a hamburger, John. What would you like with it?"

Good, I thought, let someone else be his slave, and they can get as much gratitude as I have received. I left and didn't look back.

Chapter Eleven

Everything seems to make sense now, to fit a pattern, but it didn't then. I was merely navigating in foreign waters, curiously aware that the old perceptions were wrong, or nonexistent, that the shoreline toward which I moved was no longer recognizable, or even familiar. My family had changed; the people of the landscape I knew were either gone, or not who I thought they were. With my father, there were aspects of his behavior that I found inexplicable; his manipulative dependency and his distrust a mystery to me.

Sometimes, I thought I had seen some aspects of these traits, in minor ways, all my life; other times they seemed to present as odd behavior magnified by stress, by age, or by loss. I wondered how much my mother had covered for him, how much responsibility she had quietly assumed while we never noticed. I saw her as the one who maintained the social connections, who tended the household, who always had an interest in others. My father was less involved that way. Still, he was always cordial, and fond of humor and story-telling.

His stories were so familiar I could recite them word for word, like a mantra, or a bit of prose. Many were funny tales about people he knew. Others were about feats of daring, a feature which he honestly possessed, a trait repeated through his life in sudden and extraordinary acts of courage: like the car crash where he single-handedly lifted a smashed vehicle off a tiny baby, saving both the child and the mother; or his rescue of trapped residents in a coastal storm—an event I witnessed as a young child. In these actions he had exhibited amazing strength and courage.

For him, I suppose, it was the kind of heroism of which he was uniquely capable—the dangerous, quickly initiated kind that saved lives. He was probably not good at the other kinds, the long, slogging confrontations with illness or disease, the emotionally draining kinds of bravery that require patience and persistence.

I don't know if I ever fully understood this then, but I knew that in the end, with my mother, he had not been able to help her in her illness, to comfort her emotionally, to offer anything but a greater sorrow that was edged with cruelty. I saw all of this then, and I wondered if it had always been there. Why had I not seen it before? Had it been merely garnished over by my father's talents?

And what of those gifts? Where had they gone? Where was his musical skill—the instruments he used to play—his drum, his trombone...all those times he used to accompany me on the piano? All the tunes I knew so well as a child because of him? Where did that go?

It was as if he let it slip away, and now he was content with sitting in a wing chair with his self-imposed dependency. I didn't know what he wanted or who he was.

"You wouldn't want me living with you?" he asked, still in the chair, staring out the window.

"Well...no." I answered truthfully. "You wouldn't want to live with me, would you?"

He shook his shoulders as though he didn't know how to answer.

"Daddy," I said slowly, "I don't think it would be a good idea for you to be living with me right now, but I do think it might be good if you lived closeby...so I could see you every day." Then I remembered, "You know, there's a cottage for sale two houses up the lake from us. It would be close enough for you to walk over and visit, take some of your meals with us. Would you want something like that?"

"No," he said definitively, the thought of moving clearly

too much to contemplate at that moment. "I'm better off here for now."

I questioned my decision silently, wasn't comfortable with my own answer, but I felt his presence in my home would be too destructive then, and that it would only add to his growing dependency. I would have reason to question that later perhaps, but then I was still naïve and simply trying to adjust to a new map of my world.

***

"Your father's doing very well," the psychiatrist said. He had invited me into his office after the session with Father who was still present and seated next to me. "He knows the adjustment will continue to be hard," he said, "but he is handling it very well. I'm proud of him."

My father looked over at me and smiled. I had to admit that he seemed more like himself lately. We had dinner that evening and he had even thanked me for the nice meal, something he rarely ever did. I saw a spark of his old humor and warmth and I felt immensely relieved. He told me he had been invited to Bob and Mary's for dinner that week, and also had seen Verna. He shared a long letter he received from Mina and talked to Lew about our house renovation plans. His mourning would take a very long time I knew, but I saw such an improvement in him that I felt hopeful again for the first time in months.

And he had been there for Mother's death; he had come home and faced his fears. He could hold onto that accomplishment, I thought, and to me. He seemed happier, more contented perhaps. I told him how proud I was of his progress. Later when I took him home we spoke of this.

"I guess I'm doing better," he said. "There's a lot I understand now that I never understood before."

"Like what?" I asked.

"Like the police," he said, "and why they were so interested in me."

Abruptly, the rational ground shifted, fell away under my feet, and I felt an old anxiety suddenly returning along the roots of my hair.

"Daddy," I said emphatically, "The police are *not, were never,* interested in you."

"Well," he said, "I understand why they used to drive by here sometimes."

"Why?" I asked, humoring him, wondering what his explanation would be.

"Because your mother had insurance with them...Here it is," he said, reaching into a desk drawer.

I read the words: Life Insurance Policy.

"See it?" he said. "See it? Life Insurance Police?"

"No, Daddy...that's a *policy*. It has nothing to do with the *police*."

He looked back at me, puzzled, and I wondered what visual or mental distortions were still playing out in his mind. But he gave me no time to ponder...

"And I never realized how you felt about me," he suddenly blurted accusingly, referring to a criticism I had made about him never being there emotionally for Mother or me...one leveled angrily after the fiasco of Ocean City.

I swallowed hard. "Well, Daddy, I guess we both said some things we didn't mean." I desperately wanted to let my disappointments go. I didn't want an argument. "You've been doing so well lately," I said, "and we don't want to go through all this craziness again. I have to leave now, but I'll see you in a couple of days."

I went to my car and started to back out the driveway. He came onto the porch and sat on a little deacon's bench, waving goodbye. I started to drive up the street, but something made me stop and turn around. He was still sitting on the porch, smiling. And I ran up to him and gave him a quick hug, then got back in the car and left.

When I got home I told Lew what the psychiatrist had

said, and that I was feeling for the first time that I could fully forgive my father, that I could finally see a way opening where he would have a more significant place in my life.

I had always been so close to Mother, but now there was time to know my father a little better. I could see him living at the lake, being nearby, having him with us on holidays, understanding more about the scars and wounds of his own life. I felt that he and I were being given a second chance. I confessed I had always believed it would be my youthful Mother who would live to be 90 and sit on a chair on the dock with me, watching sunsets. Now I saw that person as my father. My resentment about his treatment of Mother finally melted away. For the first time in months, I felt hope.

***

It was an early Sunday morning and the phone rang. 9AM. I was making breakfast, standing in my housecoat and slippers, and I didn't answer. I was tired. If it's important, I thought, they'll call back.

At 11AM, it rang again, and this time it was Bob. "I walked over to visit John this morning and the house is locked and no one answers." His voice sounded deeply worried. "I banged on the door a long time, but I don't have a key and I didn't want to break a window.....I thought you should come down."

"We'll be right there," I said.

As Lew and I hurried out the door I wondered: Could he have fallen? Did he take too much of his medicine? Did he oversleep? Or was he ill? I considered all of this, yet there was something more, that fey sense again of something unknown, something....I stopped myself from speculating and tried to push back my growing anxiety.

Bob was outside the house, waiting, pacing on the front porch. I'd never seen him look so distressed. Lew sprinted to the front door and used our spare key, the one given by

Mother. We called to my father, going quickly from room to room. Everything was distractingly tidy, pristine as if it had just been cleaned, nothing out of place. The hard candies I had left in a bowl at Christmastime still sat in the middle of the kitchen table. The house looked spotless and spare.

Suddenly, I heard Bob calling from the garage. I ran down there to see him standing on the steps leading to the basement. He looked shaken and frightened, the door to the basement slightly ajar. I wondered what he had seen. "I think John's down there," he said. "I don't want to go in."

I started down the steps but Lew blocked my way. "I don't think you should go down, Belva Ann."

"No, I'm going," I nearly screamed, grabbing his arm. "It's my father."

I pushed open the door then and saw what Bob saw, the soles of two shoes, a man laying in front of the washing machine at the end of a long basement. There was a shotgun on the concrete floor beside him—and God only knew what else—I ran to the figure, knowing that I was running to something, coming closer to something horrifically unimaginable. I stopped and saw the most unforgettable image that I would see in my life: my father in a fetal position, the muzzle of a shotgun inches from his head, a small red cup of blood pooling in his right ear, and a splattering of blood on the green carpet where he lay. His eyes were fixed and staring, mouth agape. I fell on my knees, gasping for air and touched his cheek. It was white and cold.

"Oh, Daddy," I sobbed...why? Why did you do this?"

He could not do this. How could he do this to himself, to me? There was no architecture to describe the pain. No words to qualify it. Nothing. But I knew, knew with a certainty that everything had shifted, all the knowns were gone, irrelevant. I could not live with it. I had failed my father. I had killed him as surely as if I'd fired the gun. I had killed him by my resentment, my weakness, my criticism, my failure to help him enough. He had gotten even, delivered a message.

He had left me with a sin for which there was no form of contrition. He had given me his last words, spoken three days ago. His desire to leave the world was greater than his desire to be in it, with me. It was over, my family was gone...

***

In the days that followed I learned that when you experience a suicide there is a suffering that surpasses by all orders of magnitude that of a normal death. A numbness and a heaviness surrounds you. It is part of the shock, an anesthesia that the mind induces to enable the stricken to survive. Reality comes in intermittent waves, like monstrous rollers washing over you with such force and power that you gasp and claw desperately at bits of flotsam to stay afloat. Then the huge waves pass and the backwash swirls you briefly between the towering swells. You drift there, shiftless, purposeless, waiting for the next assault of painful memory, the next wave.

People come and peer at you from the remote safety of their lives. They throw you platitudes and subtle life-rings of sympathy. They shake their heads and speak in whispers, "Did you hear how they found him? Why do you suppose he would do such a thing?" Or, "Poor girl...how much more can she take?"

You wear your struggle silently, and you carry on by sheer will, but the storm has overwhelmed you and no one sees. No one sees the soul adrift, the tear in the fabric of your reality, the place where healing cannot reach. For a suicide is a crime against the self, but it is also a crime with many accomplices and many victims. The guilt is vast and wide. My parents' friends, their neighbors, all felt ashamed. What if they'd done more, tried to see my father more? I could hear their pain, their own sense of guilt and failure. They looked to me for comfort, and I could give none. I could only mouth words, repeat that this was not their fault, that no one knew he was this depressed, not even the psychiatrist. He believed he was doing well; I believed he was doing well. We were wrong.

The house still had the metallic smell of the Haldol, as if he was still there, breathing unseen among the rooms. I wondered if he had taken his medications as he said he was doing, or if he had suddenly fallen into such a depression that nothing could pull him back, or worse, if he had somehow planned this all along. Lew had taken the guns from the house back in October, after the debacle of the trip to Ocean City...so how had he gotten the gun?

In the basement, Lew found the answer. He remembered stopping at the house one day in the fall and seeing my father on a stool, fiddling with the acoustical ceiling over the pool table. My father said at the time that the tile sometimes popped out of place, and Lew accepted his explanation. But now we looked again.

"I feel something up there," Lew said, reaching as far back as he could. I watched as he pulled out several boxes of shotgun shells and placed them in my hands. "He must have put the gun up there before we took your mother home with us," Lew said.

I stared at the bullets, and I felt anger suddenly cresting over my sorrow. "How long did you plan this, Daddy?" I silently asked of the empty space where he had lain. "How long?"

***

It had been only six weeks since we buried Mother and now there was another funeral. I simply recall the ground, the same heaped scar in the earth where my mother was placed, the same still-raw mound with gashes and runnels and cracks cut through it, one that had frozen, thawed, and refrozen again. Another coffin was lowered as we stood in the spitting snow, Liz holding me on one side; Lew on the other.

I heard my mother's voice then, and the words of Robert Lowell...

> *And again I looked at the snowfall*
> *And thought of the leaden sky*
> *That arched o'er our first great sorrow*
> *When that mound was heaped so high...*

We stood in a little circle. I thanked the mourners for being there. They came back to the lake house where I had listlessly prepared some cakes the day before. Lew's parents were with us from Pittsburgh. I wandered about dazed.

A distant relative took me aside. "You know, you shouldn't be so upset," she said. "This is not a tragedy. Your father was old, and he did what he wanted to do. But what happened to your friend's son...now that was a tragedy." She looked at me reprovingly. I knew she was referring to the death of a nine-year-old boy with cancer just a week prior to Father's suicide. Lew and I knew the family well.

I suppose I was unfamiliar then with comparative suffering and the pain such judgments create. I only knew then that I felt diminished, my father's life trivialized, and I was left as guilt-ridden in my mourning as I was in his death.

But she was apparently not satisfied, or finished. "And I think it was wrong of you to let people know that your father was a suicide. You shouldn't have let the minister tell them that. You should have tried to protect his memory."

I was staggered. Did she expect me to lie? And I had not even done a funeral correctly? I pulled away from her critical stare. I wanted to put miles between us, but I couldn't then. I simply fled to the kitchen, just in time to hear Lew's father critiquing the food and the shabby quality of the box cakes I had made. It was all too much. I stumbled outside in the cold. I didn't know it but my friend George was trailing close behind me.

"What's wrong with those people?" he said angrily as the snow touched his gray hair.

"I don't know, George. Lew always says some people are just socially inept or ungracious. I was wiping my eyes."

"Socially ungracious? What the hell does that have to do with it? This is a death, not a garden party!"

I don't know why his words meant so much, but I suspect it was the first time anyone had validated my feelings about such critiques in a way that I truly heard. I felt better as I hugged George and I rejoined some of my friends then. I only wanted to be present with caring people, not to have to make conversation, but I heard someone behind me...

"Oh, Belva Ann, I need to talk to you." It was an acquaintance of my mother, one vaguely remembered from years ago, and she got right to the point.

"Your mother's settee," she said, "you know, the large one at your parent's house, in the den?"

"Yes...?"

"Well," she continued, "it belonged to my mother, and she gave it to your mother about thirty years ago."

"Uh-huh. Yes, that was nice of her."

"Well, I'd like to have it now." She waited. "It used to be in our family, you see."

Something foreign and defensive rose up inside of me. "I'm sorry," I said, "but it's been with us for as long as I can remember. It was Mother's. She loved it and I want to keep it."

The woman turned on her heels, not pleased, but I was past caring about massaging egos, or giving the small treasures of my parents' life away. I returned to the living room and sank into the sofa and stayed there till the conversation around me ceased and I looked up to realize that I was, at last, alone.

***

Collapse. There is no other word for it. It was, in that winter of 1984, a state of being, one in which I appeared to function on the outside, but inside I was brittle. Empty. I only experienced a narrow range of emotions: despair, guilt, and then anger. Despair because I saw no future; guilt because I felt responsible for my father's death; anger because he had done this destruction to himself, and to me.

"I never saw a family fall apart as fast as this one did," said Mary, sadly and often, whenever I saw her. She didn't intend to be hurtful, yet her words stoked all my guilt. I wanted to scream, *But I didn't fall apart...I tried to help...I tried to keep things together!* But in the end, of course, I had failed too, and now I was plunging into a depression so deep that I could not separate it from the all-encompassing grief and shame I carried in me.

It didn't matter; such distinctions didn't matter. I only knew that I didn't know who, or what I was, what my family had been—because at the last there was a destruction so out of character, so unthinkable, that I couldn't accept it. Everything I believed had shattered. Perhaps there are greater soul wounds than a suicide—even a seemingly recriminatory one—but I had no discriminations or judgments then. I knew I simply could not live with the knowledge of my responsibility. The pain was just too great.

It was always part of my nature, a certain fragility. As a child, I had always been told I was too sensitive. I could not bear to see an animal hurt. I snuck around the house as a kid, setting off mousetraps so the mice would not be harmed; I wept over birds that fell from nests and buried them with little wooden crosses to mark the tiny graves; I rescued stranded crabs and skates and conches beached on the tideflats. When my mother tried to squash a household bug, I would run to catch it under a mayonnaise jar then release it in the yard. My father stopped deer hunting because of my distress. Now I had hurt him, failed him, and he had taken his life.

During those dark days a million "what ifs" presented themselves to me in the middle of the night: What if I had brought him to live with me? What if I had seen the big red flags in his paranoia of the police? What if I had answered that phone call at 9AM, and what if it was my father? Now I could only wonder about that for the rest of my life. And I could never know the answers, could never go back, never alter the history, then or ever. And I could not bear living with it.

I slept for 14 or 15 hours a day, getting up only when Lew came home at 6 o'clock. I would make dinner and we would talk a couple of hours, usually with me going over again and again the trauma that happened, and with Lew dutifully listening as if hearing my questioning for the first time. His willingness to let me talk was the thin thread that kept me sane. It kept me going till the next day when I would ask the same questions, re-examining my guilt all over again. Yet he never told me to "get over it," never said I had grieved enough, never told me not to speak of it. And in this, he was a shining blessing in my life, and a lifeline.

***

Three months after Father's death, I had not dealt with my parents' house. I had done virtually nothing. I needed to dispose of their possessions, clean, sort, and organize items before the auctioneers emptied the property. I had no emotional energy for anything that required personal interaction or creative thought, but I could no longer delay cleaning out the household.

I thought it would be just physical work. I needed to wade through it, to see what was there, to sort papers, letters, loose photos and albums, clothing, and all the memorabilia of our family's life together. However I was not prepared for the emotional turmoil, the profound reminiscences such actions inspire.

For several weeks I struggled through, going from room to room, looking in desks and bureaus and storage trunks as

I went, boxing the personal items I wanted to keep. But the place I could not go was the basement.

It was probably inevitable as the house grew barer in a cheerless and lifeless procession of ways, that I knew I needed to finish my task in the place I most dreaded. There were items stored in cupboards there, things I needed to see. You could call it the end of a journey, the last act of shutting down a household after death. I'm not sure how I framed it, but it was a final step in saying good-bye, the last thing left to do, and I wanted to do it alone.

Chapter Twelve

The basement always had a damp, mothball smell, a trace of mold and of things long stored away. I went down the same steps I had descended just three months before, the ones that had led to a devastation beyond imagining. He was gone, but I could still feel his presence there, maybe in my mind, maybe in the blood-stained carpet that no one had cleaned. It was like going into a catacomb or a tomb, the tiny windows curtained and admitting no light.

I felt for the light switch on the chain by the door, and realized the bulb must have burned out. I walked a few steps in semi-darkness and pulled the cord for the fluorescent fixture over the pool table. It flickered on as I looked up to see the acoustical tile still slightly askew in its metal frame, the place of hiding. I tapped it with my fingers and it snapped down into place, then I looked quickly away.

There were cupboards about the room that my father had built when he and my mother bought the house 15 years ago. I began in the corner, opening doors, peering inside them, rummaging my way around, putting a few items on the pool table.

The dishes from our summer cottage—old Willow Ware plates and Ironstone platters, appeared along with my grandmother's chipped Yellow Ware banded mixing bowl.

Far in the back of one shelf I found a heavy plaster of Paris paperweight with shells embedded in it, a kind of man-made fossil. As a kid I had proudly fashioned it for my mother, and it probably weighed over five pounds. She had saved it all these years. It nested among some drawings I had made in third grade, and some painted coasters and woven potholders I had given her as handmade gifts as a child.

On a nail high up inside the cupboard hung a piece of old stiff leather. There was writing behind it on the beam and I stretched up on a small stepladder and tried to read it. It was my father's handwriting... "October 11th, 1955, Topsey." It was the date my cocker spaniel died. He had kept her collar for thirty years. The leather was cracked; the buckle rusted and corroded from her swims with me on those beaches of Sea Isle. It still smelled of Topsey, and I sank down on the ladder, holding it against my chest, seeing her furry blackness scampering through the waves.

She was my beloved childhood friend. She would sit on the end of the sidewalk at precisely 3:30 every day and wait for my bus. But one day she was not there. What she saw, and why she ran into the road remains a mystery, but my father immediately left work and drove her to the vet where she had emergency surgery. Topsey remained in Dr. Wynn's care for a week, and she lived. The vet charged one-hundred dollars. My father made forty dollars a week, working as a mechanic in the decorating department of the glass plant, but I don't think there was ever a question in his mind that Topsey was worth it, because I loved her. He did this for me. And he had remembered her all these years with the little shrine on the wall.

I put the collar in a box and wrapped a bit of tissue around it, moving it to the side of the table with the other items I intended to keep.

I looked around the shelves and boxes, wandering aimlessly among the old Christmas decorations, the saved wrapping paper, plastic picnic plates and tablecloths, the delaminating wooden salad bowls and ceramic Easter bunnies. It was all so common, so unremarkable, and yet the essence of my parents' lives seemed embedded more surely in these simple possessions than in the fine pieces I had so carefully saved. It was here, I thought, here was the deeper life within the life...my father's old trumpet and trombone, Mother's knitting needles and crocheting tools, the set of iron horseshoes he taught me to throw, a bamboo fishing pole, and a wooden checkerboard we used in the evenings at Sea Isle.

Stories lived here; stories of years, of vacations and gatherings, holidays and friends, of common joys and bitter losses. Each thing I touched seemed to hold a memory, an album almost—of images and sounds—faces, places, and time.

In the last cupboard I came across the bag, one that held a battered black tin lunch pail. I hadn't seen it since I was a kid...my father's old metal lunch box. I lifted the lid and instantly saw my mother's hands, remembered how the sandwich and an apple would fit inside just so. My mother packed it every morning as we ate breakfast, and I saw my father go out the door to his job at the glass factory in Millville. It was grueling work, the labor physically hard and the days long. Near the liers where the hot glass bottles emerged from the furnace, the working conditions were horrendous. I suppose in winter the heat was tolerable, but in summer it was nearly beyond endurance.

After I worked at the factory two summers when I was in college, I better understood a small part of what he must have suffered. This was the end of the industrial revolution in a small factory town, and I think the conditions then weren't much better for the workers than those of coal miners. Yet my father had persevered, and because of his toil I had been able to go to college and have a better life. How could I forget what was staring at me in that black lunchbox?

I climbed off the ladder and stumbled to the place of the blood-stained rug where I involuntarily fell on my knees. I simply had no reason to go on and I felt that I could not live. My father was gone, and it was in some ways my fault, my responsibility.

I suppose I was not a spiritual person then. Beliefs were never that important to me. I was distantly comfortable with ambiguity, with a nebulous sense that the Universe, the world, was an essentially unknowable entity—perhaps divinely inspired; perhaps an accident of colliding chemicals. It seemed unnecessary to me as a younger person to commit to either point of view. Certainly, I was happy enough to please my mother and go through the motions of traditional religion, which for me was my background as a Presbyterian, but I was not sure what I really believed. So you could say I had no philosophy, no imprimatur, and no certainties. But I can remember as I crumpled to the floor that a part of me asked for something to intercede, even though I had absolutely no belief in such intercession. I asked, and I asked without believing. I told my father I loved him and forgave him; I prayed he could forgive me. I prayed for Christ to intervene. I prayed on the floor until the basement windows grew dark and until I had no more words to offer. I was drained. Around me there was only silence.

Then I realized that someone must have come into the basement while I was unaware. I felt a light pressure under my arms, two hands placed there and gently pulling me up. I believed that Lew had come in, and as I began to rise I looked over my shoulder. There was no one. The room was empty.

I was standing then, looking at the space around me, searching for an explanation, looking down at the blood-stained carpet, seeing what I thought was the greatest wound of my life, but feeling inexpressibly at peace. Something, someone, had lifted me up. As I look back on it, I still cannot explain it, cannot fully name it. Yet I know that my entire life since, that peace, has never left me.

I walked out of the basement then, carrying the boxes with me, and the old collar, the lunch pail, the Willow Ware and all the tattered remnants of family and memory. But I was not the same person who had entered that day.

As I drove home, I puzzled over what had happened—the change I was feeling—and the words "Amazing Grace" played in my head, an old spiritual I loved though I had never given much thought to the words. But on that day, for the first time, I thought I understood it—the grace that can come at the moment of our deepest despair, the grace that surpasses understanding, the grace that I always thought was poetic metaphor and not a gift of life. Whatever I had experienced, whatever healing and grace had been granted, I knew only one thing: it had not come from anything in me.

Chapter Thirteen

In May, I stood in the emptied out shell of my parents' house. The auctioneers had divested it of all its remaining contents the day before. It seemed symbolic to me of life itself—the house a container, like our bodies—of dreams, plans, struggles, years— and then the life flees and an emptiness is all that remains.

In my mind I could still see where everything had been: my mother's desk with its stack of *Lady's Home Journals* and letters, the leather holder where she kept her pens, the painting beside the desk done by her friend Kay, the photo of my grandfather on his oyster schooner next to the hutch cupboard and its compliment of cut glass and painted dishes, the blown glass ruby vase on the round table under the picture window—the one where she always displayed her summer roses, my father's fake leather recliner that had the perfect impression of his body embedded like a bas-relief in green naugahide, bottles of Old Spice on his dresser, the pink jewelry box on Mother's highboy...everything as it had been.

Now it was scattered, the few things that remained in my possession like displaced shells one carries home from the beach, while the greater shoreline of their life has gone.

The auctioneers were thorough. Nothing was left behind. I went from room to room, looking for the last time. A young family had bought the house and they would know nothing of what had been here. They would make their own memories.

It had been exactly a year since the phone call from Dr. Reiser, exactly 12 months since the territory of our lives had altered so irretrievably. How little time there is, I thought, to understand, to love, to make things right, to weave the intricate, fragile tapestry of life. We are profligate with time, believing that there's always another day, another tomorrow—and then the tomorrows end and we are surprised, stricken, as though we never saw the darkness on our shoulders.

The auctioneers had no such qualms. They were the vultures of the broken habitations, the opportunistic feeders who scraped and gleaned and pecked clean anything left behind.

In my mother's bedroom only one thing remained, a bit of litter really, something that implied the haste with which they must have worked. It lay there, in the center of the room, a tiny pink plastic rosebud, dropped on the floor where her dresser once rested. I remembered the little basket of fake blooms that gathered with it. Somehow, one had escaped its woven confinement and stayed behind.

How she loved roses! How considerate of her to remember...

I placed it in my coat pocket, knowing in my heart she would be okay, that they were both okay, then I closed the door, locking it for the last time.

Postscript:

I have written of a destruction, of a crisis at the end of life, of a time of loss. For me, this was the passage through the darkness of my family's final hours, and I made a promise, to myself, that one day I would write it down.

What I learned over the course of years is that healing takes a long time and it is not entirely linear. For me, what began on a basement floor was followed by a succession of small steps, of movement forward and backward, of ups and downs, of learning to understand my past, to live gracefully with hurt and loss and sorrow.

So it was that I gradually found my way back into my studio again, into a life as a teacher and painter and wife, into a thousand small loves and duties and pleasures that define each of us as an individual. I was passionate again about my work and found meaning and joy in it. I loved my husband and knew that he had helped me immeasurably by his listening and patience. And I was blessed by my friends, and especially Mina, who were there to soften the days and to help me in the hard time ahead.

This was all a very long time ago, yet the peace that began on a cold floor in a long distant house has never left me. It has rather enabled my life. It has given me a sense that I am part of something larger than the reality with which we customarily define the world. I may seek it, yet not find it or explain it, nor fully give it a name, but I know we labor and struggle and breathe our first breath and will suffer our last under its presence.

My parents will always be enigmas to me in some ways, perhaps as I too was to them, but I know they were fully human: kindly, loving, hurtful, generous, forbearing, dismissive, and flawed. They were all of these things, capable of them all, and at the end of his life my father fell to the worst of his fears and to the ravages of mental disease.

It was a time of loss, of enormous fracturing as I saw my family falling apart from within and without. Yet I was the overly responsible only child who assumed the care and accountability for all. And in this I was overwhelmed and consumed.

Sometimes now, when I look back on that time, I don't recognize the person I was. I would like to think that I have grown, but I realize that life is not configured like that, that crises and sorrows can always present themselves and overtake any of us. It is only by grace that we stand at all.

And so for me, when I think of them, I now feel only love and immense gratitude for all they sacrificed, all they gave me. In the end, I would like to think that is really all there is, all that matters.

When I go to my studio, when I paint the skies, I think of my mother, standing on a lonely beach, watching a sunrise in September. When I see the sled in the barn, I think of my father, pulling me through the snows of Christmas, or I hear his tenor voice when I sit at the piano and play the old songs we both loved. I remember that my own time here is brief, and the best way I can honor their love is to use the gifts that they so generously gave me.

I know the darkness is always there, at our shoulder, waiting to weaken us, waiting for its moment. But it's what we do with the broad landscape of our lives that matters, and not the weakness or frailty that may come at the end.

As for my parents, they rest in peace now beside the quiet marshes of Leesburg: John Adams Penn, and Belva Tozour Penn. I will remember them always, with gratitude, and with love.

My parents and me, 1954.

My beautiful mother in her teens and twenties.

My father and me (age 5) in our garden.

My father teaching me to ride my first two-wheel bike.

Me in third grade.

My mother's first car.

My father in his thirties with his dog, Duke, in front of the house where I grew up.

My mother with me (center) and my best friend, Sherry Brown, at our first dance in 6th grade.

Mother and me (age 15) at the beach we loved.

My mother, myself, and my father on the deck of the beach house we rented that last August of their lives, 1983.

Myself, Enjoué, and Lew on the dock of the lake house.

My parents, 1980.

Mina, 1985.

Me in the lake house studio, 1985.

About the Author:

Belva Ann Prycel is a native of Millville, New Jersey, who grew up near the Delaware bayshores and Atlantic coast of which she so often writes. A graduate of Rowan College, an artist and former teacher, her paintings have been exhibited in museums, colleges, and galleries throughout the U.S. In 2001, she was one of four artists profiled in a New Jersey Network Public Television presentation, "Bayshore Artists: Celebrating Our Sense of Place."

Prycel has illustrated two books and was a frequent cover artist for *South Jersey Magazine*. Her writing has appeared in regional magazines, environmental journals, and two national anthologies.

In 2002, she moved to Sheepscot Village, Maine, with her husband, Lewis, and their dogs, Jolie and Tucker. Since that time, Prycel has written and illustrated three books of nonfiction, *Times and Tides, Water Tales,* and *Passage*, all memoirs of the coast and of her family. She currently enjoys painting, writing, living near water, and playing ragtime piano.

She may be contacted at baprycel@roadrunner.com.

www.ingramcontent.com/pod-product-compliance
Lightning Source LLC
Chambersburg PA
CBHW052053070526
44584CB00017B/2152